Praise for David Houle and Jeff

"David Houle and Jeff Thomas Cobb have penned an accessible volume that makes the urgent case for a transformative shift in schooling and that sketches a vision of what a shift might look like. Drawing on their expertise as futurists, they persuasively and passionately argue that deep-rooted norms need to be fundamentally rethought. Their vision of what the next decade might hold and their assertion that student-centered, progressive instruction is the way of the future are sure to spark smart discussion. This energizing volume will engage educators, policymakers, and parents wondering what the next decade may hold for schooling." —**Frederick M. Hess, Director of Education Policy Studies at the American Enterprise Institute and Author of** *The Same Thing Over and Over*

"We can't educate the leaders of tomorrow with yesterday's education model. Houle and Cobb offer a much needed, action-oriented, transformative vision for what K–12 education must become. It's time to stop talking and start doing. Our future depends on it." —**Rafael Pastor, Chairman of the Board and CEO, Vistage International, Inc.**

"*Shift Ed* is a call to action. There's no doubt that David Houle and Jeff Thomas Cobb have identified where education must go, so the question becomes how will we—as parents and educators and community leaders—get there? *Shift Ed* is the kind of book that makes us ask the toughest questions about how we're educating our children today and provides a broad vision for changes we simply have to start preparing for and making today." —**Tim Sullivan, Founder and President, School Family Media, Inc.**

"*Shift Ed* is a vital work that should be read by every American interested in the future of K–12 education and the urgent need to transform and position our schools for success in the twenty-first century. . . . Buy this book now and form a discussion and action group within your own community." —**Richard J. Noyes, former Associate Director of the Center for Advanced Engineering Study, Massachusetts Institute of Technology, and former K–12 Educator**

"The strength of this book is the strong case the authors make for change. They point out how our nation is falling behind in the quest for global supremacy and what changes need to be brought about for that problem to be corrected." —**Randel Beaver, Superintendent, Archer City ISD, Archer City, TX**

"*Shift Ed* challenges your educational mindset without being intimidating. I spent the entire read asking myself, 'Why not?'" —**R. Jon Frey, Assistant Principal, Columbus High School, NE**

"*Shift Ed*'s major strength is awakening Americans, especially the educational community, to the reality that change is here; we must prepare our young scholars for a global society as opposed to past teaching and learning practices." —**Belinda J. Raines, Principal, Northwestern High School, Detroit, MI**

"David Houle has again used his vision as a futurist to identify the need for transformation in education as he has so profoundly done for us in business. *Shift Ed* is a must-read as it resonates on many levels including as a citizen, taxpayer, grandparent, and family to passionate educators observing the frustrations of the system that can't effectively compete or function in today's Shift Age." —**Wallace B. Doolin, CEO, Black Box Intelligence**

"As an urban educator passionate about transformative international education, *Shift Ed* strikes a deep chord. It is a bold call to action to ensure universal student success in a globalized environment that is ever-changing." —**Ellen Estrada, Principal, Walter Payton College Prep, INTEL Star Innovator School 2010, Goldman Sachs Foundation Prize for International Education 2007**

SHIFT
ED

SHIFT ED

A CALL TO ACTION FOR
TRANSFORMING
K–12 EDUCATION

DAVID HOULE
JEFF COBB

CORWIN
A SAGE Company

CORWIN
A SAGE Company

FOR INFORMATION:

Corwin

A SAGE Company

2455 Teller Road

Thousand Oaks, California 91320

(800) 233-9936

Fax: (800) 417-2466

www.corwin.com

SAGE Ltd.

1 Oliver's Yard

55 City Road

London EC1Y 1SP

United Kingdom

SAGE India Pvt. Ltd.

B 1/I 1 Mohan Cooperative Industrial Area

Mathura Road, New Delhi 110 044

India

SAGE Asia-Pacific Pte. Ltd.

33 Pekin Street #02-01

Far East Square

Singapore 048763

Acquisitions Editor: Arnis Burvikovs

Associate Editor: Desirée A. Bartlett

Editorial Assistant: Kimberly Greenberg

Production Editor: Cassandra Margaret Seibel

Copy Editor: Gretchen Treadwell

Typesetter: C&M Digitals (P) Ltd.

Proofreader: Jenifer Kooiman

Indexer: Terri Corry

Cover Designer: Scott Van Atta

Permissions Editor: Karen Ehrmann

Copyright © 2011 by Corwin

Printed in the United States of America

Library of Congress Cataloging-in-Publication Data

Houle, David.

Shift ed: a call to action for transforming K–12 education/David Houle, Jeff Cobb.

p. cm.
Includes bibliographical references and index.

ISBN 978-1-4129-9296-1 (pbk.)

1. Educational change—United States.
2. Education—United States—Evaluation.
3. Education—Aims and objectives—United States.
4. Education and state—United States.
5. Educational planning—United States.
I. Cobb, Jeff. II. Title.

LA217.H66 2011 370.973—dc22 2010051856

This book is printed on acid-free paper

11 12 13 14 15 10 9 8 7 6 5 4 3 2 1

Contents

Acknowledgments

There are many people to thank and acknowledge for their role in the creation of this book. First we must thank all those people who have shared their wisdom and allowed it to be shared here for the reader: Ian Jukes, Steve Turckes, Mark Greiner, Darryl Rosser, and Tony Wagner. Second, we thank those who have both led and worked in the trenches of education and have shared their visions for change: Jim Rex, Peter Renwick, Janice Mattina, and Karen Woodward.

Thanks must be given to Salvador Serrano, whose research greatly helped this book, as did the research of Melanie Kahl from Perkins+Will.

We thank those people along the way who influenced us and opened our eyes to what was right and wrong with today's educational landscape. There are many of you who have touched us, and we thank you.

To Arnis Burikovs, senior acquisitions editor at Corwin, who heard a speech and saw a vision of a book and then gave us the opportunity to write it. His guidance was instrumental and essential. To all his colleagues at Corwin who helped us bring this book to market to hopefully start the transformation of K–12 education.

We thank you all and hope this book proves worthy of your support.

PUBLISHER'S ACKNOWLEDGMENTS

Corwin gratefully acknowledges the following individuals for providing their editorial insight and guidance:

Randel Beaver, Superintendent
Archer City ISD
Archer City, TX

Victoria L. Bernhardt, Executive Director
Education for the Future
Chico, CA

R. Jon Frey, Assistant Principal
Columbus High School
Columbus, NE

Michael Jacobsen, Superintendent
Weber School District
Pleasant View, UT

Belinda J. Raines, Principal
Northwestern High School
Detroit, MI

Joy Rose, Retired High School Principal
Westerville, OH

We dedicate this book to all those educators, parents, elected officials, and businesspeople who have already begun the early stage of educational transformation and to all those who will join in this essential and noble effort. We dedicate this book to the thousands, tens of thousands, and hundreds of thousands of individuals who will come forward to face the future of educational transformation and birth it into being. Thank you in advance for making the journey.

—D. H., J. T. C.

To Victoria, with love and appreciation for your support and understanding during the writing of this book, thank you!
To Christopher with love, may your children be educated in the new ways called for in this book.
To Jordan with love, for showing me the leading edge of the digital native student and how much change must occur.
Finally in memory of my father, Dr. Cyril O. Houle, a leader in adult education who coined the phrase "lifelong learning" and wrote numerous books on education; your commitment to the improvement of education has inspired me to this day.

—David

To my wife, Celisa, my partner in life and learning.

—Jeff

Introduction

In the revelation of any truth, there are three stages. In the first it is ridiculed. In the second it is resisted and in the third it is considered self-evident.

—Arthur Schopenhauer

The book you hold in your hands is about the future of education. Specifically, it is about the future of K–12 education in the United States. We started this book with the premise that this part of the education system is broken and needs fundamental change. In recent years there has been a growing sense of failure, frustration, and acceptance that what exists no longer serves our children, our society, our country, and our place in the world. This was our departure point. The structures, ideals, and systems of education in the United States were all created in prior centuries and have not kept up with advances made by the rest of society.

There has been much debate about what to do, where to go, what matters, what is missing, and what is wrong. There have been many wonderful books and articles written about what is needed for education to provide value in this new century. There are many great thinkers who have led the conversation to help us all see what isn't working and suggest what might be done to improve education. Our purpose here is not to compete in any way with these thought leaders or the work they have done, but rather to join the conversation more from the perspective of the ordinary citizen, parent, and businessperson to provide a vision that is as broadly accessible as possible.

We are now entering the second decade of the twenty-first century and the second decade of a new millennium. We are transitioning through one of the most dynamic periods of change in human history—a time we call the Shift Age. With our growing ability to connect, communicate, and collaborate globally, the speed and scope of change seem to increase daily. But as society races ahead, our approaches to educating its youngest members—and the resources we dedicate to this purpose—seem to continually lag behind. In this book, we share with you our view that nothing less than transformation will succeed in changing this situation. We cannot repair, reengineer, or retune: we must reinvent.

We begin the journey toward transformation with an overview of how we evolved to our current state and a brief look at the many signs that the legacy education system we have inherited is now failing our needs. There is no denying that problems of education today are huge and we discuss a number of dynamics that we must address head-on if we expect to achieve fundamental change. But the goal of the book is not to get bogged down in pointing out current failings and challenges. We move beyond these to offer our vision of why transformation is necessary, what it looks like, and key areas we should focus on to lead it.

We are also fortunate to be able to offer in these pages the visions of a range of stakeholders—from architects to school administrators to businesspeople—who were kind enough to share their thoughts on the future of education. Some of these visionary comments are interspersed between chapters as brief "Change Visions." Ones we have collected from individuals currently working as administrators and teachers within our school systems are grouped together in Chapter 6.

There are two major undercurrents that run throughout the ideas offered in the book. The first is that transformation is inevitable. With or without us, the vast array of changes that new technologies have created in the past decade will push us toward a sort of *phase transition,* to borrow a term from physics. In a phase transition, there is a moment when matter suddenly shifts from one form to another in a way that seems almost magical. Think, for example, of water suddenly becoming steam when the right temperature is reached. We see an analogous shift coming in the world of learning and education. The question is whether we will be ready for the shift—whether we can help to lead and guide this coming change or whether we are simply overtaken by it.

The second undercurrent is that we already have much of the knowledge and capability we need to lead the transformation. Just as steam is fundamentally still water, *transformation* does not materialize out of thin air: by definition it is based on existing forms. Already there are numerous bright spots and pockets of change across the educational landscape, but we have yet to assert our collective will to make a true shift toward transformative change. Indeed, while there is widespread discontent with the state of our current educational system, there has yet to be widespread engagement across the general public in asking and answering the questions critical to making things better. It is time to engage. It is time to make an active, collective choice for change.

We offer this book to you with the hope of inspiring that choice and the action that will follow, for first and foremost this book is intended as a call to action, as a catalyst for creating the new vision of education for this century. It is time for that vision. It is time for transformation. It is time for Shift Ed. Please join us.

A Quick Look Back

Education is a social process. Education is growth. Education is, not a preparation for life; education is life itself.

—John Dewey

In the 235 years since declaring independence, America has grown and assumed a leading role in the world based upon the vision, dreams, and opportunity it offers: the vision to create a great nation that stood on the shoulders of great nations of history and looked forward, the dreams of freedom for all under a new form of government based upon the high ideals of citizen participation, and the opportunity to create oneself anew and forge a life of attainment and happiness for self and family.

While a wide range of factors has contributed to success in realizing our collective vision, dreams, and opportunity, one of the most essential has been the strength of our systems of public education. The evolution and advancement of the nation has gone hand in hand with broadening access to high-quality schooling for its young. For most of the past century, we have viewed ourselves—and for the most part, rightly so—as leading the world in producing highly educated citizens and workers capable of meeting nearly any challenge. But there is a growing concern—one we have heard voiced by parents, business leaders, educators, and friends and colleagues from all walks of life—that we are perhaps not as up to the challenge as we once were, that America's existing educational system is not capable of supporting the country's future evolution and advancement.

To understand why this concern exists and why it is valid, it is important to grasp fully the extent to which human society has changed over time and the dramatic shifts that have occurred just within the past few hundred years. The history of the United State has taken place over four centuries, and during that brief period, the countries that now form the developed world have shifted from social and economic systems based on agriculture, to ones based on industry, to ones based on information. As David has argued in *The Shift Age,* a precursor to this book, we are now hurtling forward past the Information Age into something else entirely. It is only by appreciating the magnitude of these changes, and the legacies we still carry with us from past ages, that we can begin to understand how to transform education for the future.

THE AGRICULTURAL AGE

Most anthropologists date the emergence of modern humans—beings with bodies and brains much the same as those we possess today—at between one hundred and fifty thousand and two hundred thousand years ago. Approximately ten thousand years ago, modern humans started literally to put down roots, and what we now refer to as the Agricultural Age began. We moved from a subsistence existence based on hunting and gathering off the land to one supported by cultivating the land. Over time, as we stayed on the land to reap the crops we grew, a nomadic way of life gave way to one more place based. This transition, in turn, led to the steadier supply of nutrition and the complex social structures and interactions that fueled additional human development. Most of what we think of as the history of humanity, and all of its developed civilizations, came into being during these ten thousand years. The basic foundation of human society, even as we still know it today, was cemented during the Agricultural Age.

During the Agricultural Age, the populations of the nations lived close to and interacted on a daily basis with the primary source of food—the land. Wealth was generated from the land and cities were formed as marketplaces for the trading of what came from the land. Understandably, the rhythm of planting and harvesting determined the entire rhythm of life.

THE INDUSTRIAL AGE

Thousands of years passed before we transitioned into the next major age in the history of humanity. Indeed, it is both remarkable and all too easy to forget that the shift from the Agricultural Age into the Industrial Age began less than three hundred years ago. Prior to the late 1700s, when commercially viable steam engines were introduced into the marketplace, the pace and culture of the civilized world remained governed largely by agricultural demands. The steam engine and a wave of other advances led to machines assuming a central role in the manufacturing of goods and the delivery of services. Products that formerly had to be produced painstakingly by hand, over many days or weeks, could be produced much more rapidly and at a much more consistent level of quality. Additionally, the use of the steam engine to power boats, and eventually trains, meant that both products and the people who made, bought, and sold them became much more mobile and connected than had ever been the case in the thousands of years prior.

The mass production of goods required large numbers of workers, and as a result, populations began to centralize and cities grew dramatically in size. Urbanization, centralization, and mechanization were forces that recast the agricultural landscape and shaped much of what we still see around us today. As the farm was the economic basis for the Agricultural Age, the factory became the foundation for the Industrial Age.

The rhythms of the world started to change and to accelerate. The bucolic flow of the seasons on the farm and in the countryside gave way to the faster paced beat of the urbanized world. Factories, as they developed and became more sophisticated, introduced increasing levels of standardization and mechanization. Other new forms of transportation like cars, trucks, and then airplanes joined trains and steam powered boats. Equally dramatic advances in communication complemented the dramatic acceleration in transportation as inventions like the telegraph and telephone shortened distances and greatly decreased the time needed to get things done. It would be difficult to overestimate the cumulative impact of all of these changes—and so many more—on our collective perception and understanding of the world. Nor is it surprising that so great a shift, and one that occurred so rapidly, left many feeling at the time—and many still feeling—that we are capable of dominating nature, rather than nature dominating us, as it had during the Agricultural Age. Inventions, discoveries, and new technological wonders empowered humanity to feel in charge of its own destiny, ever less reliant on the variable rhythms of the land.

The apotheosis of this age for the United States came in the twentieth century, when it was widely felt that America defeated the Axis powers in World War II not just on the battlefield but on the factory floor. The explosion of industrial capacity and capability the war fueled flowed into the postwar era, resulting in material wealth on a scale and breadth unprecedented in world history. America was seemingly the proof that Industrial Age practices, carried to their logical ends, could provide widely and systematically for a higher standard of living, one well beyond the reach of our ancestors in the Agricultural Age.

Of course, it is worth noting that the Industrial Age did not end the activities or the broad cultural sensibilities of the Agricultural Age; it just subsumed them within a new economic, cultural, and social order. The mechanization and increased productivity of the new age brought tremendous gains, but the new focus on standardization, quantity, and speed that enabled these gains was in stark contrast to the much smaller scale and individualized approaches to living that had characterized the Agricultural Age.

THE INFORMATION AGE

While the period of time from the early stages of the Agricultural Age to the beginning of the Industrial Age spanned many thousands of years, the gap between the Industrial Age and its successor spanned only a couple of hundred. In the United States, the roots of this new age began with the explosive growth in the number of college graduates due to the G.I. Bill after World War II. This growth led to office—or white collar—workers exceeding the number of factory—or blue collar—workers in 1957.[1] The late wonders of the Industrial Age, the radio, the television, the mainframe computer, and the first satellites in space ushered us into what is now commonly called the Information Age.

Even with these early technologies, it was clear that economic power based upon the production of goods, though certainly continuing, was giving way to wealth based upon information, communication technology, and knowledge. Any doubts about this shift began fading with the introduction of the personal computer in the mid-1970s, followed in the coming decade by the rapid widespread adoption of cell phones, fax machines, cable television, and the Internet. The amount of information in the world increased exponentially, as did the velocity with which it moved around the world. As Nicholas Negroponte put it in his 1995 book, *Being Digital*, we were rapidly moving from economies based on atoms—the building blocks of material goods and services—to economies based on bits—the building blocks of digital goods and services.

The Information Age was in full maturity as the United States and the other developed countries of the world entered the current century and we wrestle with its impact even as we move beyond it. Indeed, we still wrestle with the legacy of each of the three major ages and the shifts that have come so rapidly over the past three hundred years. As we consider the current state—and the potential future—of our educational system, we must do so with a clear understanding of how it has been impacted by our experiences in the three ages.

AMERICAN CHILDHOOD EDUCATION THROUGH THE AGES

In last thirty years of the 1700s, when the United States was formed, the Industrial Age was just beginning in England. This meant that the founding fathers of the country, and all its citizens, were products of the Agricultural Age. Its rhythms and culture shaped their thinking. The wealthy in America, as throughout the rest of the world, were the landed gentry. Many of the founding fathers were farmers and the majority of the population worked on the land. Well into the 1800s, given that the story of America was expansion westward, the settling of the land meant the farming of the country.

It was clear that the children of the new country needed education. This usually meant that a small town had a single school with a single teacher who educated children in the proverbial single room schoolhouse. Since the source of wealth was farming, the formal education of the young—to the extent it occurred at all—was structured around this economic reality. The school year was structured around the rhythms of agriculture. Children were let out of school in the early afternoon so that they could go home and help with the chores of the family farm. The school closed for a short time during the planting season—a spring break—so that the children could help on the farm at this critical time. A long break over the summer, of course, was essential as it allowed children to both play in the warm weather countryside and to help with all the work on the family farm during this critical agricultural season. School began again in the fall when the harvest season was winding down. It is this Agricultural Age school calendar that educators of the Industrial Age inherited, and while many other aspects of school have changed, it is this calendar that is essentially the one in place in the United States today.

The Industrial Age took hold in the United States in the second half of the 1800s and was initially centered in the northeast part of the country. (A more advanced industrial economy is often cited as one of the reasons the North was able to defeat the largely agricultural economy of the South in the Civil War.) This new age brought with it the factories and the cities that, by 1900, had become the hubs of economic life across the country. Standardization, centralization, mechanization, and mass production became the economic metrics of the country—even more so as the Ford Motor Company introduced the assembly line and the scientific management principles pioneered by Frederick Winslow Taylor were widely adopted as an approach to efficient production. As school came to be seen more and more as a training ground for employment, it was natural that variations on these and other industrial concepts would find their way into the developing school systems of the day.

By the end of the nineteenth century, the single room schoolhouse with a single teacher had been largely superseded by larger, more institutionalized schools—more and more of them public. It would be misleading to say that schools were consciously and actively trying to emulate factories. Rather it was a drive toward creating a "common" school experience, based to a large extent on efforts by Massachusetts's reformer Horace Mann, that shaped the school experience as we now know it. Nonetheless, it is no coincidence that schools built in the early 1900s looked "institutional" as institutions were becoming the new constructs of the age, and educators

were increasingly aware of the need to produce skilled workers capable of playing an active role in these institutions.[2] Just
as factory workers were assigned to specific roles and tasks,
children became segregated by age into grades. Days became
divided into periods. Bells, similar to the bells and sirens of
the factory, marked these periods. One teacher covering all
subjects gave way to many teachers each covering one or two
subjects. Instead of the teacher reporting to the village elders
and parents, they started to report to the centralized educational structures of principals and superintendents.

When we look at the structures, both actual buildings and
bureaucracies, of education today, they still largely resemble
this model created during the one hundred years after the end
of the Civil War. We have simply bolted Industrial Age operations and infrastructure onto an Agricultural Age calendar.

In addition, when we look at the general curriculum that
children matriculate today in K–12, it is largely the one that was
created in this same one hundred years: the three Rs; various
categories of history; a foreign language; science classes; social
studies; and some craft classes such as shop, cooking, and
perhaps a music or art class. This was the curriculum of
Industrial Age America, to prepare children to become mod-
erately educated citizens who, if they did not go on to higher
education, could nonetheless become productive adults in
this mechanized, industrial society.

In the last twenty-five years of the 1900s, the Information
Age began to influence education in the now delineated
grades of K–12. Film gave way to videotape, language labs
were created, classrooms—at least some of them—started to
have computers in them, and audiovisual elements became a
more integral part of the classroom experience. The new technologies that were shattering old business models and rede-
fining culture crept slowly into the institutional buildings of
K–12 education. The rise of the Internet—and more recently,
developments that have made the web a powerful tool for
collaboration, communication, and learning—have brought

increasing pressure for schools to be "connected" and to address the variety of challenges and opportunities that connectivity brings. This was the unfolding reality as America's schools entered the current century, and the landscape, as we know, continues to change quickly. Even the few schools that were "state of the art" in 1999 and 2000 have become out of date as wireless and mobile technologies along with myriad other advances become a common element of students' lives outside of school.

So here we are in the second decade of the twenty-first century with an education system for K–12 based much more in past than in present reality. We have a school year that was developed in the Agricultural Age to serve the economy and culture of that time. We educate our children in buildings that were constructed largely in the Industrial Age, in factories where a child enters the production process as a five-year-old in kindergarten and comes off the production line as an eighteen-year-old high school graduate. We have technologies in these education factories that are now outdated and woefully trailing the cultural and economic realities outside the school.

When we remember that our current reality is the product of changes that have occurred with breathtaking speed over the course of only a few generations, it is understandable that we are still attached to the views and practices of past ages. But the time has come to throw off the yoke of history. We can no longer educate our children, the future of our or any country, in such a legacy-bound way. It is essential to face forward and completely reimagine K–12—and beyond—education in America. The rapidly developing realities of the twenty-first century and the role that America can and should play in them necessitate a complete transformation of the K–12 educational experience.

This book is a call to action to create a completely new vision of American education.

KEY POINTS

- There have been three ages of modern humanity: the Agricultural Age, the Industrial Age, and the Information Age. These past ages have entirely shaped K–12 education in the United States and around the world.
  - o Our current school calendar is a legacy of the Agricultural Age.
  - o The rise of schools as an institution parallels the rise of the factory in the Industrial Age.
  - o Information Age changes to our school, while some certainly have occurred, lag behind the changes that have occurred in society as a whole.

- This legacy-based educational system from the past is outdated today and will not serve the needs of the future.

2

The Current Landscape of Education in America

The only thing that interferes with my learning is my education.

—Albert Einstein

"K–12 education in America today is broken."

"Colleges today have to have a full set of remedial classes as students entering college from high school these days are ill-equipped to face the rigors of a college education. Our educational system has failed them—and us."

"The young adults graduating from high school today are ill-prepared for the modern workplace."

"We are losing our competitiveness in the world because our kids are falling behind those in other countries."

All of these quotes come from individuals who have spoken to us as both parents and concerned, working adults. The first speaks as a frustrated member of a school board. The second is from a college dean who is discouraged that his school continually has to cope with the inadequacies of public K–12 education. The third speaker is a CEO whose company faces ongoing problems with filling jobs with properly educated high school graduates. The final speaker is reacting to statistics showing how American students are slipping lower and lower when compared to students in other developed countries.

The perceptions these individuals offer are common ones in the nationwide debate about the state of our education system. It is widely believed that our public education system is broken, that we are not adequately preparing our children for college or for the workplace, and that America is in danger of losing its leadership role in the global economy.

One way to frame the problem is to consider the rate of change of major institutions in our society. The argument can be made that while the speed of change in America and the world greatly accelerated since World War II, the K–12 experience and process did not. K–12 education has hardly changed at all while the culture, society, and business environment of the country have undergone changes of incredible scope and magnitude. These larger changes sped by the K–12 institutional experience, rendering it woefully out of date.

The great futurists Alvin and Heidi Toffler, in their book *Revolutionary Wealth*, commented on the relative speeds with which social institutions change. First, they suggest the metaphor of a cop sitting on the side of the highway pointing his radar gun at the oncoming traffic. "On the highway there are nine cars, each representing a major institution in America. Each car travels at a speed that matches that institution's actual rate of change."[3] They then go on to list, from fastest to slowest, the rates of speed, providing descriptions on each one. The following list summarizes the institutions and their relative rates of speed, as the Tofflers see it, but we strongly suggest also reading the full discussion of education in relation to other institutions in *Revolutionary Wealth:*

100 mph	The company
90 mph	Civil society including NGOs
60 mph	The American family
30 mph	Unions
25 mph	Government bureaucracies and regulatory agencies
10 mph	The American school system
5 mph	IGOs or international or intergovernmental agencies
3 mph	Political structures in developed countries. (Congress, the presidency, political parties)

Of the American school system, the Tofflers write:

This one shudders along with a flat tire and steam coming out of its radiator, slowing down all the traffic behind it. Is it possible it costs $400 billion to maintain this broken heap? . . . Designed for mass production, operated like factories, managed bureaucratically, protected by powerful trade unions and politicians dependent on teachers' votes, America's schools are perfect reflections of the early twentieth-century economy.

They then go on to ask the rhetorical question: "Can a ten-mile-per-hour education system prepare students for jobs in companies moving at a hundred miles per hour?"[4]

This book, of course, is based on the idea that the Tofflers' views, as well as the perceptions of the individuals quoted earlier, are valid. This chapter offers evidence—much of it quite startling—to support this view and also to further emphasize the gap that now exists between historical ideas and infrastructure and new global realities.

A SYSTEM OUT OF SYNC

Every year since 1999, Gallup has polled the general public in the United States to assess satisfaction with the current education system. The average satisfaction level over that time period has been 46 percent, and in the past five years it has varied only from 44 percent to 46 percent.[5] A national poll conducted by Leo J. Shapiro & Associates as part of the research for this book produced similar findings. When asked whether our schools are preparing children "for the challenges of a range of potential changes that may occur in the coming decades," only 22 percent of five hundred respondents indicated strong agreement that they are.[6] Clearly Americans have a sense that something is not quite right with how we are educating our children. As it happens, there are plenty of data to support that feeling. Here are just a few examples:

- Our high schools experience dropout rates of 30 percent nationwide, 50 percent in many big cities, and 60 percent or more in the lowest-performing schools.[7]
- Almost two thousand high schools across the country graduate less than 60 percent of their students.[8]
- Approximately 70 percent of all entering ninth-grade students read below grade level.[9]
- The Partnership for 21st Century Skills reports:
  - In reading, only 38 percent of White students were proficient on the 2007 National Assessment of Educational Progress (NAEP), compared to 12 percent of Black students, 14 percent of Hispanic students, and 15 percent of low-income students.

o In mathematics, only 42 percent of White students were proficient on the 2007 NAEP, compared to 14 percent of Black students, 17 percent of Hispanic students, and 17 percent of low-income students.

o In science, only 39 percent of White students were proficient on the 2005 NAEP, compared to 7 percent of Black students, 10 percent of Hispanic students, and 12 percent of low-income students.

o In writing, a skill in particular demand in business and higher education, only 41 percent of White students, 16 percent of Black students, 18 percent of Hispanic students, and 15 percent of low-income students reached proficiency on the 2007 NAEP.[10]

There is no shortage of additional evidence to make the case that American schools are not meeting even the most basic expectations we have for them: that they produce high school graduates competent in reading, writing, and math. And there is increasing concern that even succeeding with these basics is not enough. As Harvard education professor Tony Wagner and others have argued convincingly, we are not, in fact, teaching our children the right skills and knowledge to enable them to succeed in a world that has changed fundamentally. We need to expand beyond a focus on basic areas like math, reading, and writing—as important as these are—to ensure that children truly know how to *think* and *communicate* in ways that will help them thrive in a new age. Wagner proposes a new skill set—a twenty-first-century skill set—that includes:

- Critical thinking and problem solving
- Collaboration across networks and leading by influence
- Agility and adaptability
- Initiative and entrepreneurialism
- Effective oral and written communication
- Accessing and analyzing information
- Curiosity and imagination[11]

But while a shift toward teaching these twenty-first-century skills—as well as mastering, once and for all, the teaching of basic reading, writing, and math—is essential for transforming education, it is difficult to imagine this shift occurring successfully in the current K–12 educational environment. As the previous chapter suggests, the "landscape" for current K–12 education often looks more like a containment area for youth, a place for kids to bide their time until they can be released into the working world, than an environment where enthusiastic young learners can prepare for life. As students age through our system, the problem only becomes worse. Youthful energy and enthusiasm decline—partly as part of a natural process of maturing, but also because of the stultifying environment of our schools—and older students often become dangerously disengaged. As Jack Jennings, president of the Center on Education Policy, put it in an August 2010 *Wall Street Journal* article, "High schools are the downfall of American school reform. We haven't figured out how to improve them on a broad scope and if our kids aren't dropping out physically, they are dropping out mentally."[12]

For those of us who did not grow up in a hyperconnected world—a "flat" world as best-selling author Thomas Friedman has put it—it is perhaps difficult to imagine just how out of sync the experience of sitting in an average classroom from early morning until the middle of the afternoon each day must seem to child who has or may soon have access to Google, a cell phone, e-mail, Facebook, and a wide range of other tools that will allow her to communicate, collaborate, and learn globally throughout her life. The world of the standard K–12 classroom, both physically and intellectually, bears little resemblance to what children are experiencing and will experience in life, and yet we continue to expect this world to graduate students who are ready for college, work, and competition in a global economy.

As might be expected, we are falling short on all three fronts.

Not Your Forefather's College

Thomas Jefferson was one of the earliest voices for universal public education in the United States, and it is one of the few areas of endeavor in which he did not achieve success. Toward the end of his life, the Virginia legislature finally approved funding for a state university—ultimately to become the University of Virginia—while cutting language in the same bill that would have provided for public funding of elementary and secondary education. Jefferson considered it a grave error that the legislature should "raise the apex of the pyramid without the foundation in the schools."[13]

While education through the eighth grade has been compulsory in every state since 1918, there is plenty of evidence to suggest that the issue Jefferson identified has not disappeared: we are not necessarily building a foundation of learning in schools that leads to success at the college and university level. Data like the following indicate that many students arrive at college unprepared, and many ultimately fail to complete a degree:

- Of the students who enroll, 42 percent of community college freshmen and 20 percent of freshmen in four-year institutions must take at least one remedial course. As a result, the nation loses more than $3.7 billion a year, including $1.4 billion to provide remedial education to students who have recently completed high school.[14]
- According to data released by ACT in 2010, only 24 percent of the 2010 graduating high school class met all four of the benchmarks the organization has determined for college readiness, while 28 percent met none of the benchmarks.[15]
- According to the U.S. Department of Education, only 20 percent of young people who begin their higher education at two-year institutions graduate within three years. There is a similar pattern in four-year institutions, where about four in ten students receive a degree within six years.[16]

Understanding why a lack of readiness for college, or post-secondary education in general, is such a critical problem requires understanding the massive shift in the job market over the past few decades. As a recent study by the Georgetown University Center on Education and the Workforce suggests, we now live in a world where the majority of *all* jobs—not just higher paying jobs—require some form of postsecondary education. The study indicates that

> between 1973 and 2008, the share of jobs in the U.S. econ-omy which required postsecondary education increased from 28 percent to 59 percent. According to our projec-tions, the future promises more of the same. The share of postsecondary jobs will increase from 59 to 63 percent over the next decade.[17]

Individuals who are not able to successfully pursue post-secondary education are at a significant disadvantage in the current U.S. and global economy. Increasingly, the opportuni-ties available to them are confined to lower paying jobs that effectively block them out of a middle-class—much less upper-class—existence.

Assuring that students have the necessary skills to suc-ceed academically when they arrive in college is essential, but it is also critical to recognize that the entire experience of col-lege has changed over recent decades and it is also necessary to prepare students for the reality rather than the ideal of postsecondary education.

Once an option for only a small, elite segment of the American population, the dramatic growth in the number of colleges and universities and the enrollments at these institu-tions since the mid-twentieth century has resulted in a much more diverse demographic for higher education. As a recent Gates Foundation study suggests, the idealistic vision many of us have of college as a place where students go for four years to diligently attend classes during the day, study at night, and attend parties and football games on the weekends is largely out of sync with reality. The study indicates that the following:

- Among students in four-year schools, 45 percent work more than twenty hours a week.
- Among those attending community colleges, six in ten work more than twenty hours a week, and more than a quarter work more than thirty-five hours a week.
- Only 25 percent of students attend the sort of residential college we often envision.
- College students with dependent children constitute 23 percent.[18]

In particular, the need to balance postsecondary education with earning a living is a reality that seems much more likely to grow than diminish. We can and should continue to push for larger amounts of financial aid to be made available to postsecondary students, but we also need to develop a vision for how work and education can become more fully integrated. In an increasing number of professions, while focused preparation is certainly needed, taking large amounts of time out from day-to-day work is likely to be harmful to a worker's skills, knowledge, and future prospects. This harm may significantly diminish any benefits the education received during that time provides. In other words, the entire notion of a defined four-year, or even two-year block for postsecondary education may be largely outdated for the vast majority of students.

Already there are many signs that a traditional college or university education may not be enough, or may not really even be the right starting point. The sophistication of corporate education programs, for example, has risen dramatically over recent decades, and an increasing number of companies have elevated the person with strategic oversight for learning to a C-level, or chief learning officer, position. There is a thriving market among trade and professional associations for certificate, certification, and credentialing programs as well as general continuing education credit. The opportunities for informal knowledge sharing and learning on the social web are boundless, and an increasing number of institutions of higher learning contribute to the available mix of content by releasing all or large parts of their curriculum as *open education* resources. MIT, for example, now provides web-based access to nearly all its course content through the MIT OpenCourse-Ware initiative. It is hardly alone in doing this: more than 250 institutions globally have banded together to contribute to the initiative though the OpenCourseWare Consortium. It is only a matter of time before effective assessment strategies are established to certify and credential the knowledge that enterprising learners gain through use of these tremendous learning and knowledge assets.

Just as we are not succeeding in cultivating either basic skills and knowledge or twenty-first-century skills and knowledge in our K–12 students, we are also not preparing them effectively for a traditional college experience or—much more important—the much more dynamic postsecondary learning opportunities and challenges they will encounter as they exit the K–12 system. The impact this lack of preparation has on business is already being felt—and it will be felt ever more strongly as the world of work continues to rapidly evolve.

Learning—and Relearning—to Work

In a blog post titled "If Truth in Advertising Was Applied to the School Motto," global education consultant Clark Aldrich offers up the following (among many others) tongue-in-cheek slogan:

> In just 12 short years, we will prepare you for an entry level job. The rest is up to you.[19]

Aldrich's words point piercingly to the failings already discussed in this chapter, as well as to the pain felt increasingly by many business leaders. Whether a child continues on to college from high school or goes directly into the workforce, one of the foundational assumptions of the American education system is that she will be prepared to do productive work. A range of data, however, suggests serious issues with the quality of skills and knowledge our high school and college graduates bring to work with them.

- The Georgetown University Center on Education and the Workforce study previously cited shows that by 2018, the United States will need 22 million new college degrees—but will fall short of that number by at least 3 million postsecondary degrees, associate's or better. The shortage amounts to a deficit of 300,000 college graduates every year between 2008 and 2018.[20]

- In a recent survey of more than 400 employers, only 23.9 percent reported that new job entrants with four-year college degrees have "excellent" basic knowledge and applied skills. In the same study, 43.4 percent of employers reported that the preparation of high school graduates was "deficient."[21]

- A recent survey of 217 employers found that half the companies provide readiness or remedial training, but most are not satisfied with the results.[22]

It is to be expected, of course, that individuals starting a new job may need training specific for that job, but for workers to show up lacking the general skills applicable to any job environment is inexcusable. A more disturbing—and almost certainly deeper—issue, however, is that this lack of initial readiness may signal a long-term deficiency with respect to workers' abilities to move from one job to the next and one career to the next. According to the Bureau of Labor Statistics of the U.S. Department of Labor, the "average person born in the later years of the baby boom held 10.8 jobs from age 18 to age 42."[23] This figure seems unlikely to decline in the coming decades. Indeed it seems likely to increase—and along with it the likelihood that an individual will not only shift jobs a significant number of times but fully switch *careers* a significant number of times.

Naturally, job shifts tend to come with new learning demands, and career shifts come with even greater learning demands. We can and should look to employers to a certain extent for helping us learn new skills and "retool," but to an even greater extent, we must be prepared with the fundamental skills necessary for guiding our own lifelong learning. The skills we acquire during the thirteen years of K–12 education should indeed prepare us for much more than an entry level job; they should fully empower us to—in a positive sense— have the rest be up to us.

Those who are prepared to learn well and learn quickly will not only be able to adjust better and survive when significant changes in the job market occur—for example, like the major wave of outsourcing that has impacted the U.S. economy—they will also be much better prepared to take advantage of new jobs that do not exist and that we cannot even foresee at this point. One of the keys to the rise of India and China as players in the global economy has been that these countries not only recognized the new opportunities that a more connected, flat world offered, they were also able to supply a large number of workers with the right skills to seize upon the new opportunities.

If we are to remain a leading force in the new global economy, we must be able to do the same.

HOLDING OUR OWN IN THE GLOBAL CLASSROOM

China and India did not, of course, produce a highly capable workforce overnight. Both are countries that have invested in the foundation necessary to "raise the apex of the pyramid" as Thomas Jefferson put it. Around the world, other countries are raising the quality level of their K–12 education and producing more postsecondary graduates while U.S. efforts in these areas remain largely unchanged.

- In the Program for International Student Assessment (PISA) 2006, U.S. fifteen-year-old students' average science literacy score of 489 was lower than the Organisation for Economic Co-operation and Development (OECD) average of 500, and placed U.S. fifteen-year-olds in the bottom third of participating OECD nations. Fifteen-year-old students in sixteen of the twenty-nine other participating OECD-member countries outperformed their U.S. peers in terms of average scores.[24]
- In PISA 2006, U.S. fifteen-year-old students' average mathematics literacy score of 474 was lower than the OECD average of 498. Fifteen-year-old students in twenty-three of the twenty-nine other participating OECD-member countries outperformed their U.S. peers.[25]
- Among the twenty-eight countries that participated in both the 2001 and 2006 Progress in International Reading Literacy Study (PIRLS), the average reading literacy score increased in eight countries and decreased in six countries. In the rest of these countries, including the United States, there was no measurable change in the average reading literacy score between 2001 and 2006. The number of these countries that outperformed the United States increased from three in 2001 to seven in 2006.[26]
- While the United States has, in the past, typically led the world in the attainment of postsecondary degrees, a 2010 report from the College Board notes that the country ranks twelfth among developed countries for the number of individuals age 25 to 34 with an associate's degree or higher.[27]

Digging deeper into most of the numbers presented here reveals that Americans do not always perform poorly in real terms on the various tests and assessments. In some cases they do, but in many cases, the issue is simply that the scores of

American participants have not improved over the past decade or more, while those of other countries have. In a highly competitive world, it is these relative standings that matter. As we have already witnessed with the large-scale migration of computer programming and customer service jobs to places like India and China, when skilled workers are available elsewhere, and typically at significantly lower costs, there are few barriers left to keep companies from employing workers wherever it makes the most economic sense.

In a very real sense, American students today study in a global classroom every bit as much as companies compete for talent and resources in a global economy and consumers shop for goods and services in a global marketplace. The skills and knowledge students develop must be consistently gauged not just against other students in the local class or even across the nation, but also against students from across the world. For all the emphasis on accountability and testing in our schools over recent years, this is a perspective that really is not taken into account. While many business leaders and education leaders may be aware of figures like those previously discussed, we have done relatively little to rethink or reconfigure our schools as part of a global classroom.

At the same time, we have also not seriously considered the possibility that the measurements we use should no longer be about how many people we graduate from college or how high we score on standardized tests. As noted, we have slipped in many areas of educational attainment more as a matter of relative standing than in absolute terms. It is only natural that as other countries develop in the way that America did a century ago, they will see a significant rise in the sort of educational attainment that accompanied our economic development. It is certainly useful, at some level, to know where we stand in relation to other nations, but there is also the danger of simply falling into an us-versus-them mentality that leaves us playing catch-up rather than leading innovation for learning in a global economy. Doing so will prevent us from developing a truly global perspective on education.

Fixing what is broken in our schools, arming students with the skills they need for continued success in postsecondary education and lifelong learning, and building a workforce that is fully capable of surviving and thriving on a global playing field—none of these goals can be accomplished without a fundamental shift in vision.

FACING THE ISSUES AND SHIFTING THE VISION

Clearly there is a great deal of work to be done, and if we are to move ahead, we approach this work in the face of a range of broader challenges that require new and innovative ways of thinking.

Financial Crisis of Funding

There is no doubt that improving education will require a large financial investment. It is estimated that to meet President Obama's recent pledge that "by 2020, America will once again have the highest proportion of college graduates in the world" would require an increase in spending of $16 billion per year,[28] and this figure does not take into account ensuring that the students who arrive at college are actually *ready* for college.

Having now come through a global recession that has eviscerated economies and therefore government revenues, there is a grave danger that we simply will not make the required investments. Debt has become a four-letter word. In the United States and around the world, government at all levels is finding itself in deficit and with declining sources of funding. Services are being cut; libraries are being closed; teachers are being laid off; parks and recreational facilities are closing or having hours of operations drastically reduced. There is a growing call to reduce spending. This situation will not change anytime soon.

The pain has already been felt at every level of education and will get worse before it gets better. Everyone is feeling the pain and therefore everyone is defending their own turf and pointing somewhere else for cuts to be made.

Special Interests Over National Interests

The divisiveness in American political and social life seems to have reached record proportions in recent years. Individuals seem more likely than ever to put the desires of a group with which they identify ahead of the needs of the larger community. In the educational systems, there are factions at war with one another. Teacher unions fight with school administrators. Tenured professors fight to hold onto guaranteed jobs while millions lose jobs in a changing economic landscape. Politicians and religious groups fight to change school curriculums to align better with their belief systems.

Charter schools, for-profit schools, magnet schools, and home schooling now join public, private, and parochial schools. Everywhere there is fragmentation, disagreement, and dissent regarding K–12 education. In the face of this increasingly entrenched collection of special interest groups we must somehow forge a unified vision of the future of education.

English as a Second Language and American as a Second Culture

Hispanics and other ethnicities have exploded as a percentage of the U.S. population over recent decades, but we have yet to truly face up to the language challenges this change presents for our educational system. In most school systems, the question of linguistic assimilation is hardly addressed, much less taken seriously. Even if the adults of immigrant families speak their native language at home, it is expected that English is the language of the schools.

And language is only the most obvious aspect of this shift. While America used to be described as a melting pot, immigrants and other groups traditionally identified as minorities are less likely than in the past to trade their core cultural values for a mainstream American identity.

There are clear challenges in these changes, but as we wake up to the reality of a globally connected world, the linguistic and cultural diversity that we find in our own culture represents a tremendous opportunity we have yet to fully embrace.

Sustainability

Sustainability, the idea that meeting present needs should not deplete future resources, was not a mainstream concept when the vast majority of our schools were built. Obviously times have changed, and in spite of the failure of the U.S. Congress to significantly reform our energy policies, it seems clear that there will be significant upheaval in the coming decades as we attempt to restructure toward a much more sustainable way of life in our states and cities.

Most of our schools were built at a time when energy was cheap and, as a result, the buildings themselves are inefficient and the transportation resources required to bring children to and from them on a daily basis are enormous. At the same time, children today are born into a world where recycling has become mainstream and understood. Unlike their parents, many children today start school with environmentally aware habits and will have little choice but to deal with sustainability as key cultural, social, and economic factor for their entire lives.

The need to face sustainability is becoming critical, and our schools represent one of the key places for meaningful change.

A Reorganizational Recession

The global recession of 2008 to 2010 is a reorganizational recession between two ages—the Information Age and the Shift Age. It marks the point at which we clearly turn from an old economy where a standardized set of skills and knowledge could serve for a lifetime to a new economy where the ability to continually acquire and refine new capabilities is the only path to success. Entire categories of jobs are being jettisoned in the United States, not unlike the period in the 1970s when millions of Industrial Age jobs were lost and the Information Age jobs had yet to replace them. It will no doubt be years before we truly reconcile ourselves to this change, and in the meantime, there will be plenty of anger and misdirected efforts to hold on to the past. This may in fact be the greatest danger we face—attempts to hold on to the past and continue teaching and training students for Industrial Age and Information Age job markets that will no longer exist.

These attempts to hold on to the past will be in vain. In the next chapter, we turn our focus to the future and consider the powerful forces that are pushing us forward whether or not we are prepared.

KEY POINTS

- Public confidence in K–12 education in the United States is low, and justifiably so according to a wide range of data.
- The data indicate that students are arriving at college insufficiently prepared and that the college experience has become quite different from the ideal of four years of focused education—many students must balance college with work and family life in order to attend college at all.
- Businesses are finding that neither high school nor college graduates are as prepared for the working world as they need to be. Significant remedial training is required to make the new employees' workforce ready.
- Our scores in fundamental areas such as literacy and math have been declining relative to the scores of students from other countries, and we now rank twelfth among developed countries for the number of individuals age 25 to 34 with an associate's degree or higher.
- In the midst of the decline in educational metrics, we are facing powerful dynamics that are altering the social and economic landscape. These include: a global recession, significant funding challenges for education, a rise in special interests, an increase in nonnative language and cultural identification, and an evolving emphasis on sustainability.

CHANGE VISIONS

From Train to Rocket

Ian Jukes has been a teacher at all grade levels: a school, district, and provincial administrator; a university instructor; and a national and international consultant. To date, he has written or cowritten fourteen books and nine educational series and has had more than two hundred articles published in various journals around the world.

Ted McCain is an educator who has taught high school students for twenty-five years. He has been an innovator and pioneer in technology education. He has written or cowritten seven books on the future, effective teaching, educational technology, and graphic design. His focus is on the impact on students and learning from the astounding changes taking place in the world today as a consequence of technological development.

Lee Crockett is a national award-winning designer, marketing consultant, entrepreneur, artist, author, and international keynote speaker. He is the director of media for the InfoSavvy Group and the managing partner of the 21st Century Fluency Project.

What follows is an excerpt from the most recent book from Jukes, McCain, and Crockett titled *Living on the Future Edge: Windows on Tomorrow.*

Education as a Train

Let us picture education as a train. It is pulled by an engine fueled by our desire to educate our children to become effective citizens and to teach them practical skills for success in the world of work. To do this, education must pull many cars down the track—reading, writing, mathematics, geography, history, government, law, languages, science, art, music, woodworking, mechanics, metalworking, and physical education, to name but a few. Today's schools have even more cars being attached to the train in the form of new and different expectations from the public of the school system as modern society continues to change.

Now we are being asked to integrate students with special needs, as well as those whose first language is not English. We have become social workers, providing counseling and shelter for students with drug problems or teenage pregnancies. We are asked to watch over those who are victims of physical, emotional, or sexual abuse. We are also asked to take on the role of surrogate parents as families break down. We are expected to build self-esteem, providing personal and moral guidance. All this, while at the same time being responsible for the delivery of a relevant and meaningful academic curriculum. Despite the many obstacles of money, mindset, and time, we are pulling the educational train down the tracks faster and more efficiently than ever before, adding new cars as we go. The truth is that educators today are doing a better job than they ever have.

So What's the Problem?

Consider the impact technology has had on modern life. Technology has fundamentally and irrevocably changed life for virtually every person in our society. It has compressed time and distance to the point where we can now see history as it happens. World events are viewed in real time, live and uncensored, simulcast on YouTube, Twitter, and e-mail. Mainstream media can't even keep up. Instead of the wire service, they are following the story as it unfolds on the web. At the same time, an army of volunteer contributors are updating the facts on Wikipedia. Now consider education in this new high-tech environment. Despite our best efforts, education is increasingly disconnected from the rest of the world we just described. Public education has had very little real competition and, as a result, it has become a virtual monopoly. Educators' responses to the dramatic changes taking place in the outside world are dulled because they approach the changes primarily from an educentric point of view. They tinker with the education system and curriculum as it exists and want to keep it the same instead of addressing what it needs to become for the benefit of the students. They need to ask, "What does a student need to learn?" instead of "What do I want to teach?"

Want proof? Let's compare a classroom in a school to a modern office. Imagine a group of workers who retired 15 years ago returning to their office. What has changed in those years? Everything! Cell phones, voicemail systems, color photocopiers, courier services, the

Internet, e-mail, global online collaboration, video conferencing, Facebook marketing, advertising on Twitter, and even the systems and the way of doing business—the list is endless. Businesses have had to invent and reinvent themselves again and again over the course of the past 15 years just to survive. Almost nothing from the old office remains except for perhaps the water cooler.

Now take those same retired workers back to the schools they attended 40 years ago and consider what has changed. While today's school culture and social environment may have changed significantly, from a structural and instructional point of view, very little, if anything, has changed. We still operate in basically the same school day, same school year, same organizational structure, and same instructional delivery model that was used 40 years ago. How can this possibly be?

This is an important question and the answer reveals much about the nature of the education system. Before we suggest why these retired workers feel so disoriented at work and so comfortable at school, let's summarize what we have said about the nature of modern life. The message has been clear from the outset of the book. Change has become an integral part of our lives. There is no question this is disconcerting for the majority of the population. Anyone over the age of 30 grew up in a much different world than that which exists today. Over the course of the last 15 years, we have moved from the late Industrial Age of stability to the Information and Communication Age of constant and even accelerating change. It's not just about change today and status quo tomorrow—it's about change today, change tomorrow, change forever.

Education's Response

How has education responded to this dramatically new technological world we have discussed? The answer is, it hasn't responded in any significant way. The educational system is possibly the most stable institution created by late Industrial Age society. Further, those inside the system have an educentric view of the world that shields them from dealing with the outside world. This sets the stage for a remarkable drama playing out in our schools today. Returning to our train metaphor, we've just added another car called technology to an already lengthy train. We have put technologically driven change in a compartment so traditional instructional activities can continue untouched.

Even though outside of education technology has profoundly affected most of the world we live in, the technology car has not had a parallel effect on any of the other cars on the education train. In many schools today, the use of technology is still considered to be little more than just another add-on. It is not seen as a fundamental and integral aspect of the education train.

While it's true this train is improving, and has even added a modern technology car, it's still a train. It's still basically unaffected by the technological developments of modern life. Unlike the rest of the world, where the power of smart devices is changing the rules of daily life everywhere, education has demonstrated an amazing stability and resistance to such change.

Why? Because many of the people inside the educational system suffer from paradigm paralysis. Like those people we discussed in the first chapter of this book, educators today are victims of their established mindset. This is certainly not to say that they are not intelligent, rather it's to say that they work in a system increasingly disconnected from the rest of world. Worse, there is little, if any, pressure to connect, let alone keep up, with the rest of the world.

This is due in large part to the fact that much of the evaluation that takes place in the school system is inwardly focused. Educators compare themselves to other educators. Such a perspective promotes the misconception that we are doing the right kind of work with students. This is the real problem facing education today. We are doing a really good job of providing education, but the kind of education we provide is increasingly irrelevant to the modern, changing world in which we live—a world driven by the exponential trends we have presented.

If education is a train, with technology in a separate car, the tracks it runs on are Industrial Age thinking. When microelectronics emerged in the late 1970s, the rest of the world left the track that education was on and took a different path.

When technological power continued increasing at a truly astonishing rate in the 1980s, the rest of the world got into an airplane called the Information Age, because a train simply couldn't go as fast or change direction as quickly as one that operates in the freedom of the air.

New dimensions, new speeds, and new directions were being developed outside education, but education stayed on its Industrial Age tracks and missed both of these important changes. It continued down the same old track, thinking that it was doing enough by improving the efficiency of the train. The net result was that education became better and better at what it was doing, but at the same time, more and more disconnected and irrelevant to what was happening outside of education.

We must realize that the education system can't continue operating this way. It can't continue to get better at delivering an obsolete education. No matter how much the train is improved, it's still a train. The rest of the world has changed. We must also change if public education is to survive. If we choose to ignore this, private industry will innovate us out of business.

The World in a Rocket

Now we face an even greater challenge. Within the next few years, the rest of the world outside education will be climbing into a rocket and heading for orbit using the new technological devices and powers that started appearing at the beginning of the new millennium. Why a rocket? And why so quickly? Didn't the world just switch from a train to an airplane?

The answer lies with the trends we discussed earlier. Many educators do not yet fully appreciate that the technology they see and use is just part of a continuum of developing technological power. While we were busy with the details of our normal lives, electronic technology has steadily doubled in power time and again over the last 50 years.

However, the real story is what lies ahead. As the saying goes, "You ain't seen nothin' yet!" As we have presented, the exponential growth in technological power is about to kick into overdrive in much the same way it did for the farmer who asked his king for grains of wheat. For the farmer, the result was an unbelievable payday when the king reached the end of the chessboard. For us, the result will be some truly unbelievable technologies. None of us are prepared for what is about to unfold. However, unlike the situation with the farmer, the doubling effect of technological power does not stop at the end of the chessboard. This story of developing technological power will extend well into the 21st century, with no foreseeable end. We are about to get into a rocket, technologically speaking.

What will this doubling effect have on our lives? Although it's diffi-cult to accurately predict exactly what the technology will look like, there is little doubt that it will revolutionize virtually every aspect of human endeavor.

What about education? Let's consider the children who are entering the school system in kindergarten right now. What kind of world will they graduate into? What should the school system be doing now to prepare them for that future? With changes of such enormous magnitude coming within such a short time frame, we can't continue to just tinker with a train that needs a complete overhaul. In fact, it may be time to discard the train. This is because fundamental and pervasive changes are required if we want education to survive, let alone be relevant, in the world of the 21st century.

Many educators know something big is happening in the world outside education today. Many even say they want a new system to meet the changing needs of the students who will live in the world of tomorrow. Still, they continue to act in the same way that they have for years. However, rhetoric is not the language of change. In and of itself, it can't transform education.

If a new system is what's needed, we must begin to do things differently. The changes we must make to the way we prepare students for the rest of their lives must be substantial. True, we won't be able to make these changes overnight, but change we must. These changes will take some time, so we need to get moving today. If education hopes to meet the challenge of preparing the students of today for the world of tomorrow, it must break out of its current mindset and move ahead rapidly to embrace the new paradigm of constant and accelerating change.

A Look Ahead

The major advances in civilization are processes that all but wreck the societies in which they occur.

—Alfred North Whitehead

The condition of our current education system must be understood against the backdrop of one of the most dynamic times in human history. The future historians of 2100 will look back on the fifty-year period from 1975 to 2025 as the time during which humanity made fundamental shifts and created new realities and levels of consciousness that did not exist prior to this period of profound change. We have already seen how rapidly much of the world has moved from the very long period of the Agricultural Age into the Industrial and the Information Ages. There will be at least as much change in the fifteen years from 2010 to 2025 as there has been in the thirty-five years since 1975.

Peter Drucker, the great management guru, wrote in his magnificent book *Post-Capitalist Society*:

Every few hundred years in Western history there occurs a sharp transformation. We cross . . . a divide. Within a few short decades, society rearranges itself—its world-view; its basic values; its social and political structure; its arts; its key institutions. Fifty years later, there is a new world. And the people born then cannot even imagine the world in which their grandparents lived and into which their own parents were born.[29]

Clearly we are now living through one of the periods of transformation that Drucker describes: during the fifty years from 1975 to 2025 human society will be rearranged—indeed, we are already well on our way. The first thirty years of this period, the Information Age, was characterized by an emphasis on information technology, much as the Agricultural Age and the Industrial Age were characterized by a focus on tools and machines, respectively. The next twenty years—the period in which we now live—is what we view as the *Shift Age,* a stage of human evolution characterized by a fundamental shift in consciousness.

We all feel a sense of shift in many if not most of the aspects of our lives. The speed of change accelerates rapidly and the scope is ever broader. Drucker's words are truer than ever: certainly those born into this time will hardly be able to imagine the world of their parents and grandparents. And it seems equally certain that these youth and their predecessors in the current generation of K–12 will feel increasingly disconnected from our approaches to learning. So why today are we educating the children of the twenty-first century in the same general manner that their parents and grandparents were educated in the twentieth century? Why are we educating the children of the Shift Age with educational constructs that were created to serve the Information, Industrial, and even Agricultural Age societies?

We have seen that education is already out of sync with current times, and has dramatically lagged behind the rapid change of society in general. Now, we will take a look at the new age we have entered, consider the essential characteristics of this new century, and suggest what lies ahead. It is this future that we must face if we are to have success in reinventing our views of education from cradle to grave.

THE SHIFT AGE

Everywhere there are clear signs that we have left the Information Age and entered the Shift Age,[30] an age when we truly come to terms with what it means to be globally connected and to master the opportunities that connectedness brings. Whenever there is a transition between two ages, there is necessarily disruption and upheaval. The "Great Recession" of 2007 to 2010 represents precisely this sort of disruption and serves as the major economic signpost for the current transition. Uncertainty has increased dramatically; economic schools of thought are in conflict—and, in many cases, wrong at the core; institutions we have long lived with are crumbling before our eyes; and we are experiencing a dynamic rate of change that cannot be directed or managed with the clarity and certainty of the recent past.

If there exists any doubt as to whether we have left the Information Age, we may simply ask, "Do I have enough information in my life?" The answer, of course, is yes. In fact, many of us probably suffer from information overload and struggle to manage the incoming rush of information in our ever more connected world. If scarcity creates value, then information in and of itself is rapidly becoming worthless. We must now move *beyond* information to find real value. For institutions that have largely been purveyors of information— and our schools certainly fall in this camp—making this change rapidly and successfully is fundamental to survival.

Embracing and rapidly managing change is fundamental to the consciousness of the Shift Age. The speed of change has accelerated so much that it is now environmental: *we live in an environment of change.* Change has become the context of our lives, not just one of the dynamics of it. We must always adapt. In business, three-year business plans are now laughable as conditions constantly change. The old phrase "standing on solid ground" no longer has merit. If an individual believes she is standing on solid ground and has a clear, certain view of the world, it is now a given that whether it be six months, nine months, or a year from now that person is going to suddenly realize the world has changed while she was busy being certain.

As already noted, education has changed at a much slower rate than the surrounding society. It was already woefully behind society when the Shift Age began. Now that change is environmental, it is essential to not build upon and update the present educational system but to leap ahead into the future and create something of and for the future.

While we have surely experienced many periods of great uncertainty in the past, a closer examination of the three core forces of the Shift Age will clarify that what we now experience is nothing less than the global stage of human evolution. Humanity has moved from family to tribe to village to city to city-state to nation-state. At least for now, our only remaining boundaries are planetary. We have entered the global age of humanity.

The Three Forces of the Shift Age

Every age is ushered in and shaped by a confluence of forces that disrupt and alter society. Computers, communications, satellites, a knowledge-based economy, and the move from analog to digital all helped shape the Information Age. In a similar way, the three dominant forces shaping the Shift Age are as follows:

1 Accelerating Electronic Connectedness

2. The Flow to Global

3. The Flow to the Individual

Of course, there are many dynamics and influences presently defining our world in the early part of this new millennium:

religious fundamentalism; geopolitical issues such as energy, poverty, migration, and resource allocation; and population growth. But these three forces—Accelerating Electronic Connectedness, the Flow to Global, and the Flow to the Individual—are the underlying, essential, irresistible energy flows that announce a new age in humanity's evolution, a reorganization of global society that rivals any in history.

Accelerating Electronic Connectedness

In the five years from 2005 to 2010, the world experienced an unparalleled growth in connectivity. At no time in human history have so many people joined the global communications of humanity so quickly. In these five years alone, more than 2.5 billion new cell phone subscribers joined the existing base of slightly less than 2 billion users. More than 2 billion people regularly log onto the Internet via computers. Most of the communications traffic now travels at close to the speed of light through the vast networks of fiber optics that were installed since the early 1990s.

The time difference between calling someone who is fifteen feet away on a cell phone and calling someone twelve thousand miles away is negligible—perhaps five seconds or less. This means *that for the first time in human history it can be said that there is no time or distance limiting human communication.* Since mobile devices are mobile, this connectivity means that place is no longer a limitation to human communications either.

Think about that: *for the first time in human history, time, distance and place are no longer necessary limitations to human communication and interaction.* Such immediacy is nothing less than transformational: we are approaching a point when an idea moves almost simultaneously through a population.

One powerful—and to some, frightening—outcome of this transformation is that we are becoming connected together into a global brain, a *neurosphere,* that vast exceeds the sum of the many brains that comprise it. This neurosphere is a pulsating, exploding, synaptic electronic place that is new to humanity. It makes possible a *global village* vastly more comprehensive and interconnected than Marshall McLuhan could ever have envisioned when he coined the phrase more than four decades ago.

Compare this current, and accelerating, connective reality to two hundred years ago when the speed of human communication was however far and fast a horse could travel in a day. It was in this reality that the fundamentals of K–12 education were created. Even one hundred years ago, when the forces of the Industrial Age were coursing through and shaping our culture, only a fraction of people—and schools—had landline phones. Place, time, and distance were physical limitations that no longer exist in this new connected landscape of today.

This Accelerating Electronic Connectedness is both creating an alternate reality and changing our consciousness. The alternate reality is the new screen reality that didn't exist with critical mass connectivity until the last ten years. The new consciousness is a global one where we are instantly sharing and experiencing events and ideas.

It is this Accelerating Electronic Connectedness that, more than almost any other dynamic, necessitates a complete transformation of education in the United States and the world.

The Flow to Global

In the twenty years since the fall of the Berlin Wall and the subsequent collapse of the Soviet Union, a new global economy has come into being. The collapse of the Eastern bloc meant that the number of potential consumers for the goods and services of capitalist enterprise literally doubled. Country after country has found its way onto the playing field of this new emerging global economy. As this change has occurred, we have begun to move further from our past geographical orientations of family, tribe, town, state, and country—though each remains important—and more toward a global orientation that is supported by the electronic connectedness discussed previously.

Historically, economics is often the initial driver of human discovery and development, followed by politics and culture. For example, Christopher Columbus did not set out to *discover* America: he set out to find a trade route to India (and Native Americans have been called Indians ever since). It was this desire for economic gain that resulted in the European discovery of America. Once America was colonized, it started to develop its own culture and, with the American Revolution, its own politics. In a similar way, the global economy in which we all now live and work will surely give birth to global culture and politics.

The global problems humanity faces today can no longer be solved by a nation-state or even several nation-states. These global problems now necessitate global solutions. Nation-states will continue to define the geopolitical landscape of the world, but increasingly there will need to be new regional and global entities to deal with the major issues we face as a species. Climate change, global financial connectivity, scarcity of water, the development and use of new sources of energy, and entire new global economic behavior patterns all point to the need for such entities.

Culturally, this new Flow to Global means the development of an ever more integrated global culture. Services like YouTube, Facebook, and Twitter, using the connectedness of the neurosphere, enable a degree of cross-cultural integration never before seen in human history. And this integration is not just happening online: the Shift Age will be time of great geographic migration. Whether people are temporarily or permanently settled in another country than their birth, this new migration will be numerically unprecedented. All countries of the world will experience an increasing amount of new cultural influences due to this human movement.

We are now in the global stage of human evolution. The Flow to Global is not good or bad; it just is and there is no turning back. This new stage demands an entirely new definition of education.

The Flow to the Individual

Even as humanity becomes more globally oriented, individuals have more power today than ever before in history. The changes that occurred in the world from 1985 to 2010 constitute the foundation for this new reality.

The explosion of choice, the growth of free agency, the technologies and dynamics that moved us from hierarchies to networks, the ever-growing electronic connectedness, and its increasing speed have all helped to shift power from institutions to individuals. Gatekeepers are disappearing; disintermediation and its primary agent, the Internet, have reorganized the economic landscape. The individual is becoming the primary economic unit, the micro that is combining with the macro of the Flow to Global. We are distinct individuals who are global citizens.

This new reality means that the age of the mass market, at least as we have previously understood it, is now over. The aggregation and organization around mass that is then institutionalized has ended. All forms of structures that are based on this model from the 1900s are in decline. We see this decline all around us. It will accelerate as we continue to experience an explosion of choice, customization, and flexibility that will allow individuals to be ever more unique and to choose their own paths, even if in small or seemingly insignificant ways.

This Flow to the Individual has brought about and will continue to bring about the decline of and, in some cases, the creative destruction of institutions that relied upon mass. The field of education is hardly immune to this force. In the Shift Age, where the power of the individual is greater than at any time in history, how can education continue to be institutional and standardized? What does standardized mean today? In a nonstandard world, in a world where institutions hold less and less power, the educational standards and approaches of past ages must cede to new forms that better serve the specific needs of each individual learner.

For many people—and perhaps even readers of this book—the full range of questions and issues that the Flow to Individual and the other forces raise are not yet obvious.

There is always a lag time in recognizing a transition as large as the one we are currently experiencing. We will see it clearly only in hindsight, but what is clear already is that the three forces of the Shift Age will have a tremendous impact on the twenty-first century. In fact, they are the beginning of the definition of what the twenty-first century will be about.

With this supersonic pace of society today we must truly and fully embrace Bob Dylan's famous line:

"Don't look back!"

The Twenty-First Century

While the transition to a new age can be subtle and occur over a number of years, the numbers on our collective calendars are exact. This book is being written in 2010, the tenth full year of the new century and the new millennium. This new century will bring more transformational change than the last millennium. This new decade might bring more change than the last one hundred years—think about that.

A thousand years ago, Europe was medieval, living in the dark ages. The world was flat, the earth was the center of the universe, and people rarely traveled beyond where they were born. Compare that reality to today. Then consider that this new millennium will bring evolutionary change at least a thousand times more transformative than the one just past.

A hundred years ago, England was the most powerful industrial country, the wonders of the industrial age were just becoming available to the general population in a limited way, and there had yet to be a world war. It was also the time when children were educated in a classroom where they sat at desks and listened to an adult teacher talk to them and write things on a chalkboard.

Marshall McLuhan once said that we drive into the future using only our rearview mirror. What he meant was that most people can talk about where they have been and tell their story: they carry the reality of the past forward. They do not look ahead or are not able to articulate where they are going. Does this not describe how education has crept forward, by always looking in the rearview mirror?

This quote is very apropos of where we have been in the first ten years of the twenty-first century. We basically continued with the legacy thinking of the twentieth century. Most of us have continued to view the world through the filter of the past. Sure, there have been the developing forces, described previously, that have forced us to think and act differently. Yes, we have become unsettled and anxious as those great institutions of the last century—such as the newspaper, the broadcast network, and the Detroit automotive industry—have collapsed and declined. But all said, most of our society still thinks and operates with twentieth-century constructs. That is about to change.

Stop and think for a minute what the phrase *the twentieth century* means to you. Depending on who you are, you might think of it as the American century, or the century of two world wars and unprecedented human destruction. You might think of it as the apotheosis of the Industrial Age, the century of science or the triumph of medicine over disease. Whatever you hold in your mind about this century began with World War I and the decade of 1910–1920. Prior to that time, the world lived in the construct of the nineteenth century: Victorian England, the four hundred families of the social register of New York, the landscape of a rural and globally noninvolved United States. It can be said that it was the second decade of the twentieth century when the definition and shape of the century began.

Living in a time when the speed of change is environmental, we must fully let go of the past except as a historical foundation. We must face the future and let go of legacy thinking.

2010 to 2020: The Transformation Decade

This new decade will be the decade when humanity begins to face the new century and leave the old century behind. The old ways of thinking, of governing, of doing business and yes, of educating our young are about to fall away. We are just now starting to truly face the problems, issues, dynamics, and unprecedented opportunities of this new century. This decade will be the time when humanity reorganizes, redefines, reinvents, and fully realizes that it is time to embrace the glories of the twenty-first century.

This decade will be one of, if not the most, transformative decades in human history. Without question, it will be the most transformative decade in the history of health care and medicine. This will be due not just to the incredible discoveries and practice we will develop, but also to the moral choices we will face for the first time. This will be the decade when our replacement parts will be an improvement on those with which we were born, when we will all know our own genetic maps at low cost, when all health care becomes personal and preventative, and when we will have the opportunity for the first time to decide who might get to live forever in an overpopulated world. How will we cope and adapt to this new reality?

It will be the single most transformative decade in the history of energy. We will begin to wean more than five billion people off petroleum with a variety of alternative and renewable energy sources. We will find new ways to create energy that are not yet known.

The accelerating, almost exponential increase in technological innovation will present realities that stagger the mind. A device the size of an iPod or e-reader will hold all the books published in a year, or in the last one hundred years. We will make dramatic strides toward forms of artificial intelligence that equal or surpass the human mind. We will have computers the size of current mobile devices that are as powerful as the large supercomputers of today. We will create synthetic life and apply these new life-forms to serve and support us.

We will approach and perhaps manifest a new global consciousness of which the visionaries and mystics of the past only dreamed.

Yes, this decade of transformation will completely recast humanity and the direction and opportunity we face in the twenty-first century. As part of the process, it is essential that we completely transform all our educational institutions, constructs, methods, and vision to keep pace. It is now time to fully embrace the potential of this new century and seek new ways to prepare our young for what lies ahead.

KEY POINTS

- We live in one of the most transformative times of change in human history. People born in the coming years will hardly be able to imagine what the lives of their parents and grandparents were like.
- We call the new age we have entered the *Shift Age,* a time when we truly come to terms with what it means to be globally connected and to master the opportunities that connectedness brings. In the Shift Age, rapid and pervasive change is an integral part of everyday life: it is *environmental.*
- The three dominant forces of the Shift Age are:
  - Accelerated Electronic Connectedness
  - Flow to Global
  - Flow to the Individual

- We have entered the Transformation Decade of 2010 to 2020, a decade of greater change than in any other decade in human history. Legacy thinking can no longer serve our purposes—and it will certainly not lead to the education system we need.

CHANGE VISIONS

The Need for New

Mark Greiner is senior vice president and chief experience officer for Steelcase Inc., the global leader in the office furniture industry. Named to this role in May 2009, he is responsible for developing insight-driven experiences to the many ways people work and wherever work happens.

A View to the Future of K–12 Education

The Need for New

In the movie *Dead Poets Society,* Robin Williams plays John Keating, a 1950s-era boarding school teacher with some unorthodox teaching methods. He has students stand on his desk to encourage them to look at the world in a different way, tells them that they are powerful individuals, and insists, "You will have to learn to think for yourselves." His methods shock other faculty members, most who teach through repetition and rote memorization. Yet Keating's methods offer key insights into the future of K–12 education.

For much of the last century, the dominant vision of schooling, exemplified by Keating's colleagues, was instructionism, a pedagogy that prepared students for the industrialized economy of the early twentieth century through memorization of facts and procedures. But the world today is much more technologically advanced, and problems are more complex and interconnected. Students need a deeper understanding of facts and procedures, the ability to critically evaluate what they learn, and to express themselves clearly both orally and in writing. Rather than simply memorizing compartmentalized, decontextualized facts via an instructivist approach, students need to learn how to integrate knowledge, and to work with ideas and concepts creatively to generate new ideas and solutions.

Just as teaching and learning face significant change, so too the classroom must change. Traditional classrooms—boxes filled with tablet armchairs arranged in rows facing a whiteboard where an instructor dispenses sound bites of information—are hallmarks of the last century and roadblocks to the current century's demands. Similar to the library, which has been transformed from a lonely book warehouse to a place where students access information and actively engage with it, the classroom as one-way lecture hall needs a drastic makeover into a place of interactive learning. Everything about a traditional classroom, from where it is positioned to how it functions, who leads discussions, and how information is shared and manipulated and new knowledge is generated, needs a thorough rethinking.

The New Process

What's driving these changes is *constructivism,* which says that it's the learner who constructs knowledge. According to constructivist pedagogy, teachers actively involve students, guiding them to construct meaning as they make their own discoveries during the learning experience. This meaning is based and builds on their prior understanding. Students learn when they construct their own meaning, not when they are being fed information through didactic lectures. This explains why students often do not learn deeply by listening to a teacher or reading from a textbook.

The constructivist teacher takes on a facilitator role. Instead of teaching *to* students, instructors help students understand knowledge and guide them to solve problems in a very hands-on way. Constructivism has been used primarily in science and math curricula, but is increasingly being applied in language courses, business courses, and others, and learning processes at all grade levels are becoming more learner centered. Students have the opportunity to learn by doing and interacting. Instructors are no longer authoritatively delivering the content by rote, but rather designing and implementing curricula that give students more control over what is learned and how it is learned, often through team-based activities that are experiential and discovery based.

The New Student

As more educators adopt constructivist pedagogies, student expectations are changing. They want the opportunity to learn actively, and they prefer doing to listening, with hands-on activities that involve familiar contexts and tasks. Young people are more community oriented in nature, value friendships more, spend less time alone, and pay more attention to peer opinions than students in past generations. None of this will be surprising to anyone who's noticed the younger generation's affection for Facebook, Twitter, and other social media.

Younger people also reveal a greater tendency toward cooperation and consensus building, and thus respond well to group activities that give them opportunities to work collaboratively, a cornerstone of constructivist theory. These students enjoy learning experiences structured in a familiar social context that relate to the students' own experiences and to real-world complexity. Newer pedagogies that are collaborative, cooperative, and project based embrace these expectations and are more likely to result in students who can relate knowledge to different contexts.

Generations

T-t-t-talking about my generation.

—The Who

G iven that the history of humanity is generational and that education is, to a large extent, driven by the need to pass knowledge from one generation to the next, a book on transforming education can hardly avoid the topic of generations. In our current environment, however, the topic is more important than it ever has been before. For the first time in history, we have entered a period where it is common for members of as many as five generations to find themselves living and working together. We may see that range expand even more as human longevity continues to increase along with the relative health of the older population. If we are going to undertake change in an area as broad as education, we must understand the roles that each generation may play.

In the last century, particularly in the United States, there has been a sociocultural elevation of generations portrayed as having distinct qualities, influences, and character. The *Great Generation* of the Depression and WWII gave way to the *Silent Generation* of the 1950s, which gave way to the *Baby Boomers.*

In each case, a generation represented a place in the history of the country that was marked both by major historical events and by ascendant cultural qualities.

It can certainly be argued that, as with all types of generalizations, generational categories are simplifications at best. Generations are made up of millions of individuals who are unique and distinct, and in many cases, generational identification may have much more to do with mindset than age. So, any discussion of generations as whole and distinct entities is necessarily a generalized discussion. That said, generalization can be a useful tool if employed judiciously. So, we now take what we hope is a judicious look at four key generations that have impacted, are impacting, and will impact education globally and in the United States for the next half century.

BABY BOOMERS: THE BRIDGE GENERATION

Members of the Baby Boom generation were born in the Industrial Age, spent the majority of their adult lives in the Information Age, and are now entering the later stages of life in the Shift Age. They represent the first human generation to have lives that touched three ages. They were born in the mid-twentieth century and are beginning to cede social power and control in the first quarter of the twenty-first century. They are the bridge generation between these two centuries as well as to the cultural knowledge of the ages not experienced by the younger generations.

The Boomers matriculated in a K–12 educational system that was fully based upon the Industrial Age model. The last of the Boomers, born in 1964, graduated in the early 1980s, when the Information Age had yet to impact the schools of the country in a significant way. They are also the dominant generation running, overseeing, or participating in the educational systems today. The vast majority of school superintendents, school board members, principals, and a significant percentage of teachers are Boomers. Not only are the ranks of school leadership filled by older leaders, there is also an upward trend in the average age for some leadership positions. A 2003 RAND study, for example, noted that from 1988 to 2000, the average age of principals increased from 47.8 to 49.3 years in the public sector and from 46 to 49.9 years in the private sector.[31]

The Boomers professionally entered the K–12 education system at a time when unions were on the rise, pensions and job security were expected, and thinking was institutional. Is it any wonder that the status quo has largely been maintained? At the same time, the Boomers brought a strong sense of ideology to established institutions and drove a great deal of change and innovation. It was this generation that led education into incorporating television, computers, and now the Internet into the classroom. The Boomer generation then, has been both the enforcer of the educational structures and a leader in change. Boomers have carried the mantle of education for thirty years and now must pass the generational torch.

As the Boomers approach the end of their generational bridge into this new century, they must cede formal leadership roles to the two generations closely following them. At the same time, as one observer has put it, "the 78 million Baby Boomers in the workforce" represent "the largest, healthiest, most accomplished generation of retirees we've ever had."[32] Assuming that they can effectively work with a younger generation of leaders, they may represent a significant resource for transforming our schools as volunteers in our communities.

GENERATION X: A DIFFERENT VOICE

While Boomers are generally characterized by their high ideals and drive to remake the world in their image, Bill Strauss and Neil Howe, coauthors of *Generations: The History of America's Future, 1584 to 2069*, argue that the generation following the Boomers—*Generation X*, or the *Gen Xers*—is much more focused on pragmatism and effectiveness. The trends toward transparency, openness, and accountability in the business world are signs of the Xers exerting considerable influence in spite of representing a much smaller portion of the overall population than their Boomer predecessors or the *Millennials* who will come after them. We can expect these qualities to grow in importance as this generation continues to move into leadership roles—including leadership roles in education.

While the Gen Xers' role as leaders will be an important factor in the direction of our schools in the coming years, their role as parents is arguably more important. Neil Howe notes that

> in the early 1990s, Gen Xers began joining parent-teacher associations in the nation's elementary schools. Around 2005, they became the majority of middle school parents. By the fall of 2008, they took over as the predominant parents of high school seniors.[33]

Because of their majority status, how Gen-X parents view the current state of schools—and their perspective on what type of change will actually have an impact—will be a critical near-term factor in both how and how rapidly we undertake the transformation necessary in our educational system.

Currently, while a majority of the general public believes that there are problems with the public education system, most parents (76 percent)[34] indicate they are satisfied with the education their own children receive in school. To the extent that they are dissatisfied, Gen-X parents have a tendency to take matters into their own hands and tackle whatever issues their own child is facing—even if that means moving the child to a different school. Getting Gen-X parents on board with broader public reforms, however, may be a significant challenge. As Howe argues, it is "practically impossible to persuade most Gen-X parents they should relinquish their choice for the sake of some great public good."[35]

It seems reasonable to expect that options, accountability, and the ability for individual parents to make choices about their children's education will be a significant focus of Gen-X educational leaders. The efforts of these leaders will no doubt help fuel significant change, but the responsibility for leading real transformation may lie with the next generation—the Millennials.

MILLENNIALS: THE EMERGING LEADERS

The Millennials are the generation that has come of age in this new millennium. They entered the twenty-first century in their late teens or early twenties and are the new generation in the workforce today. They have much different values than their Baby Boomer parents and have been the first adult generation fully shaped by the Information Age from birth.

Millennials have spent the better part of their lives, since adolescence, on computers and digitally connected. While they are the second largest segment of the general population in the United States (26 percent) behind the Baby Boomers (33 percent),[36] they are the largest segment (30 percent) of the Internet population. As near-native users of the web and digital technologies, their expectations about communication, access to information, and the options for learning are intrinsically different from those of prior generation.

In broad terms, Millennials have been characterized as "confident, self-expressive, liberal, upbeat and receptive to new ideas and ways of living"[37]—a description that may suggest they have much in common with their Boomer parents. But while some observers have labeled the Millennials the "me generation"—a term also often applied pejoratively to the Boomers—others argue that its members may, in fact, have more in common with the G.I. generation—or Great Generation.

A 2008 *Washington Post* article characterizes the Millennials as a "civic" generation—a type of generation that stands in contrast to the "idealist" generation represented by the Boomers. "Because idealist generations are unwilling to compromise on moral issues," the article's authors argue, "they've always failed to solve the major social and economic problems of their eras." Civic generations, on the other hand, "react against the idealist generations' efforts to use politics to advance their own moral causes and focus instead on reenergizing social, political and government institutions to solve pressing national issues."[38]

The last generation that fit this description was that of Franklin Roosevelt, and the transformative impact of that generation on the world is widely recognized. As Eric Greenberg argues in *Generation We,* there is good reason to hope for something similar from the Millennials; Greenberg characterizes the generation as

> not pessimistic or vengeful. Rather, they are sober in their view of the world. They believe in technology and know they can innovate themselves out of the mess they are inheriting. They believe in entrepreneurship and collective action, and that each person can make a difference. They are about plenitude, and they reject cruelty. They are spiritual, responsible, tolerant, and in many ways more mature than their predecessor generations. They reject punditry and bickering, because they are post-partisan, post-ideological, and post-political. Most important, they believe in the greater good and are ready to dedicate themselves to achieving it.[39]

Whether the Millennials will live up to this kind of rhetoric remains to be seen, but certainly the types of traits Greenberg describes are exactly what are needed to successfully guide the transformation of education. It is from this generation, of course, that the next wave of new teachers, coaches, and budding administrators of K–12 education in the United States will come, so its members necessarily will play a key role in making any transformation happen. Whatever their other qualities, the fact that they have significantly less attachment to the structures, culture, and viewpoints of the Industrial Age is likely to be a significant driver in producing change. The Millennials can see more clearly than any other generation the huge disconnect between the current education system and the world around it. Additionally, they are closest to and therefore best prepared to understand the generation that follows them, the generation that is and will be the students of the K–12 educational system now and for the next twenty years, the *Digital Natives.*

DIGITAL NATIVES: TODAY'S AND TOMORROW'S STUDENTS

Digital Natives are the first generation *born* into the digital world, the first generation to spend their entire life living in the digital landscape. They are eighteen or younger. They cannot remember living in a house that does not have a computer, or at least having access to one. They cannot remember when mom and dad didn't have cell phones. They have experienced television as a portal of dozens if not hundreds of channels. They cannot remember not having access to the Internet. They are the first generation to be able to text on their first cell phones in childhood.

The Digital Natives are the current students of K–12. They will be the students in K–12 for the next twenty years. They are the very first generation of all that follow to spend their entire lives in a digital world. They therefore are worth watching closely as they represent the current and future students of all our educational institutions.

First, we must accept how different they are from the Baby Boomers and Generation X. Both of these generations are immigrants to this new digital landscape. Just as immigrants to a new land have always had to struggle to understand a new language, new social customs, new ways to communicate, and a new culture, the Boomers and Xers have, to a widely varying degree, struggled to cope with the new digital world they inhabit.

Anyone reading these words who is a parent of a teenager has experienced this difference. Anyone who has a child under the age of ten knows that once the child has been shown how to turn the computer in the home on, that is just about the last instruction needed. Compare that to digital immigrants who often need constant tech support, help, and guidance. Think about the fact that the Digital Natives are the first generation to personally interact with a computer in childhood. That alone has transformed them relative to any preceding generation.

The Digital Natives usually get their first cell phones or smart phones between the ages of ten and fourteen, or during middle school. Baby Boomers got their first cell phones in adulthood. Digital Natives have spent, are spending, and will spend their childhood with the entire world and everyone in it just a few keystrokes away. They have access to more knowledge typing on their keyboards than the most connected scholars in the world had twenty years ago, and certainly more than the greatest scientists of the world in past centuries. Never in human history have children had access to the knowledge of the world until the Digital Natives.

People from older generations sometimes argue that the Digital Natives have short attentions spans and are incapable of focused, deep concentration. But to a large extent, they are simply taking advantage of what is available to them. If all of us older than the Digital Natives had grown up with most of human knowledge available to us within several keystrokes, might we not have also developed a similar habit of constantly searching and moving rapidly from one experience to another? The negative view of this habit is that it signals inattentiveness; the positive is that it represents a high degree of interactivity and engagement with the world. This interactivity plays out constantly in the ability of Digital Natives not simply to receive information passively from traditional media sources, but to seek out the specific knowledge they desire. This is the first generation that has fully experienced the word *search* as both noun and verb as an integral part of childhood. Again, parents of a child currently in K–12 know that their child seems capable of multitasking and casting attention across multiple screens and platforms in a way that they find impossible. This child's entire approach to experiencing the world is different.

Short messaging technologies and social media such as MySpace, Facebook, and Twitter have provided the Digital Natives with an opportunity to constantly connect with "friends" with no restrictions of time, place, or distance. This is the reality of their environment. Having become accustomed to living in this environment, they find it hard to imagine less, much less to accept less. It is no wonder that they can tend to tune out in an Industrial Age classroom when an adult from a prior generation tells them to turn off this connectivity to the world so that they can concentrate on the monotone voice of a single adult for forty-five minutes. If the world is connected, then it could be said that a nonconnected classroom is *not* of this world. At least this is the way the Digital Natives view the situation, whether consciously or unconsciously.

The Digital Natives are the current and future customers of K–12 education. It is they who will shape the future of America for the next forty years. Since they are the first of all subsequent generations to be born into a fully digital land-scape, it stands to reason they will, in adulthood, be trailblazers in ways we can only imagine. Indeed, the ways in which they go about knowing the world may, in fact, position them to be some of the most effective learners that humanity has yet produced—assuming we are ready for them. As Marc Prensky, originator of the term *Digital Native* and author of *Teaching Digital Natives: Partnering for Real Learning* has put it,

> Ironically, it is the generation raised on the expectation of interactivity that is finally ripe for the skill-based and "doing-based" teaching methods that past experts have always suggested are best for learning, but that were largely rejected by the education establishment as being too hard to implement.[40]

Those of us committed to transforming K–12 education in America for at least the first half of the twenty-first century must strive to help the Digital Natives realize their full potential by providing learning environments and experiences that fully capitalize on their native attraction to interactivity and learning by doing.

The first three generations discussed in this chapter—the Boomers, the Xers, and the Millennials—must face the challenge and embrace the opportunity the Digital Natives present as one of the initial steps to the transformation of K–12 education, and all forms of education in America. As a critical component of this process, we must involve the Digital Natives deeply in the change. We must remember the lead time it will take to create the hundreds and thousands of new schools in America. A full mobilization of resources will still make this process last twenty years. By that time, the Digital Natives will be part of education as teachers and principals. Getting their input now might not be a bad idea.

KEY POINTS

- We are living during a unique point in history in which more generations than ever are living and working side by side. The four generations key to the near term efforts to transform education are the Baby Boomers, Generation X, the Millennials, and the Digital Natives.
- The Baby Boomers represent a bridge to the past, to the legacy we have inherited. Their ideals drove many of the progressive changes to education in the second half of the twentieth century. Boomers may be a tremendous resource for education as they retire from the workforce.
- Generation X has brought a pragmatic voice to both business and education. Its members are assuming, and will continue in, educational leadership positions for years to

come, but equally important, they also represent the majority of parents of school-age children and in that role must serve as a force for change.

- The Millennials are the next generation of leadership and may represent the true force for transformation. They have been characterized as a civic generation that combines some of the ideals of the Boomers with the pragmatism of the Xers.

- The Digital Natives are today and tomorrow's students. They are the children of the Shift Age and instinctively embrace many of the forces for transformation with which older generations struggle. It is critical for them to have an active voice in leading the transformation.

CHANGE VISIONS

Reconnecting

Darryl Rosser is both a CEO and an innovative thought leader in American education reform, committed to transforming public school classrooms for twenty-first-century learners. As president and CEO of Chicago-based furniture company Sagus International, Rosser has been featured by both 20/20 and Time *magazine as a CEO that exemplifies "corporate consciousness and compassion."*

Education in America is broken. And I don't say that lightly. It's a big problem—the importance of education for our kids is not only essential for their future, but for ours as well, and the future of America.

It is clear that something needs to change if the future of K–12 education stands a chance. How do you fix something that is broken? You change it. While there has been much discussion about "twenty-first-century education," it is frequently just used as a buzzword without really talking about change. I believe that the future of education calls for change in the form of entirely new kinds of learning environments.

The problem is so large and the need to change so important that I think it is critical for the private sector to roll up its sleeves and take an active part in helping to initiate the needed fundamental changes.

Sagus International, a company that manufactures furniture largely for schools, is in a position where we can influence and have a significant impact on improving education in America to define the optimum learning environment that will improve results in education. As CEO, this has become my personal mission to understand the needs of today's schools, and to work directly with educators, students, and other thought leaders to create an environment that will enhance America's competitiveness in education achievement.

In my studies, I found little collaboration between the various parties engaged in creating the educational system. Much thought was placed on curriculum, charter schools versus public schools, teacher training and motivation, technology, budgets, and architecture. Furnishings were almost always an afterthought. In planning schools, I found also a real disconnect between the U.S. Department of Education, State Department of Education, and the local districts. Great pride is taken at the local level to design schools to meet their budgetary requirements as defined by their bond issue. Best practices from around the country are usually not considered. Collaborative team planning by all parties is usually not performed with administrators, teachers, students, architects, technology providers, furnishings suppliers, textbook publishers, medical and community leaders, and leaders of afterschool programs. Each of these groups must be given a seat at the table to fully collaborate on creating the new twenty-first-century K–12 educational experience.

Historically, there is a significant disconnect between the private sector and the public sector in solving the American education dilemma. Local businesses will throw a few "PR dollars" at their community school, but on a national level, business typically looks at education as a government problem. On a business proposition basis, companies cannot see the immediate payout or benefit of engaging in improving education. The varying levels of government and administrative bureaucracy do not make it easy for businesses to become involved. Those who do attempt to engage usually give up in frustration after a few attempts to add value.

All of that said, as a CEO, I have found it to be an extraordinarily satisfying experience in engaging with schools to help them to enhance their learning environment for students. We have engaged with a number of teachers and administrators who care deeply about their students and their ability to advance in life through a solid education. When we have been able to cut through the red tape and be impactful at various schools, it is heartwarming to see the looks on the students' faces. It is for them like opening a Christmas present. But even more important is to see the impact on their learning experience. We are all affected by our environment. At work, if we work in a disorganized, run-down dump, we will perform at a different level than if we work in a well-planned office environment with all of the correct tools to perform our jobs. Over the years, I have been engaged in the turnaround of a number of companies. In all cases, I have found that to achieve the best results, an environment conducive to great performance must be created; this of course entails having to organize, demand, and expect great results, and to give the team the tools to achieve success. It is no different in our schools.

Beyond the personal pleasure we receive from our engagement in the transformation of education, the knowledge we have gained has been impactful in our business development and in designing new products to fit the future of education—products that are flexible and mobile, budget sensitive, ergonomically compatible with today's learning requirements, and environmentally friendly. But more significant than the specific product design characteristics, the most important element is to assure that the furnishings are integrated in the overall school plan.

We will continue our journey to engage with the education community on a national and local level to enhance the education system in America. America's success depends upon a strong education system. We encourage others to join us in this, and we encourage the educational administration to embrace private support. This problem is too big for one group to handle alone.

Why Transformation Is the Only Path

Those not busy being born are busy dying.

—Bob Dylan

trans·for·ma·tion/ˌtræns fərˈmeɪ ʃən/—noun

1. the act or process of transforming

2. the state of being transformed

3. change in form, appearance, nature, or character (n.d.)

As the previous chapters suggest, education does not simply need to be changed; it needs to be *transformed*. While new policies, curriculum updates, more training and increases in salaries for teachers, and better approaches to testing may all have a significant impact, they seem unlikely to produce the more fundamental shift that is needed. There are two key reasons why we must prepare not for incremental adjustments or restructuring, but for a deep-seated change in the form, appearance, and nature of our educational system.

The first reason is that "pouring new wine into old bottles" will only have so much impact. The teaching of new skills sets geared for the twenty-first century is essential—and should be embraced immediately—but if our institutions themselves are flawed, if we are as badly out of sync as we seem to be, how far can we really get by working within old paradigms? We have tried for decades now to introduce reforms into schools that recapture the glory days of education in the early industrial era, but these efforts have failed again and again to hit the mark. Indeed, they have often led to new problems and the need for yet more reform. We need new paradigms and an entirely different way of looking at the role education plays in our society.

The second reason we must prepare for transformation is that it is most likely unavoidable. The forces we have discussed and the sheer speed and scale at which they are impacting us make it highly likely, if not inevitable, that our lives will change dramatically in the coming decades. These forces are coming at us like a truck barreling down the highway and now that they are in motion, there is little chance that we can stop them. The question is not whether they will have a transformative impact, but whether we can take the wheel and direct them toward the best possible future.

We can't know what our destination will look like any more than the Wright brothers could have foreseen all of the details of modern space travel, but we can begin to articulate a vision for how our educational system must change in its form, appearance, and nature.

A Change in Form

The form of school right now is a box: boxes on a calendar, box buildings, box classrooms. Boxes suggest borders, boundaries, and neatly defined spaces and ideas, but in a world where borders and boundaries are increasingly blurred, where ideas flow and change with a speed unmatched in history, boxes are not the form upon which our schools should be based, physically, psychologically, or intellectually.

Indeed, the extent to which schools should have a standardized form at all is perhaps one of the biggest questions with which we need to wrestle as we consider the future of our educational system. The question is partly about buildings and physical architecture, but it is more about nonbuildings and nonphysical architecture. As we have the increasing freedom to access knowledge and educational resources through the web, mobile phones, and other sophisticated communication devices, we have to question what is gained—and what is lost—by confining our children within four walls for preestablished periods of time to be fed content that fits within a predefined set of measurements.

The common perspective on computing these days is that it is moving into *the cloud*—a place where data and applications are no longer confined to a specific server box but are distributed across a far-flung network infrastructure. Whether the cloud is the right metaphor for education remains to be seen, but it is clear that we need to do much more than simply rearrange the chairs in our classrooms or knock down a few walls. *We need to break out of the box entirely.*

A CHANGE IN APPEARANCE

The appearance of schools aligns with the form. You know when you drive by a school. It stands apart; there is usually a great deal of brick and asphalt, and significant fenced-in areas. The only other type of building with which you are likely to confuse it is a prison.

While the world has always had its solitary philosophers or small bands of teacher and followers, the idea that learning is something so completely separate from the activities of real, everyday life and work is relatively new one. For childhood education in the United States, it is primarily a vestige of the

Common School movement that took root and grew with the Industrial Age. There are, of course, very good reasons why a democratic society would want to provide a "common" standardized education for all of its children. Indeed, the move to common schooling and the establishment of a strong curriculum in reading, writing, and arithmetic was one of the key factors that led to the rise of America as a global power in the first half of the nineteenth century. But the common approach does no favors if it becomes—as it has—more about the institution than the outcome.

How a school looks may seem like a trivial detail in the grander vision of education, but we all know intuitively that our surroundings—how they look, how they feel, the moods and attitudes they support—have a great impact on our day-to-day lives. And a growing body of research suggests that over the long term, they can have a tremendous impact. Why would we expect that shipping our children off to drab, confined, linoleum-paved containment areas each day would result in the types of motivated, creative individuals we need to carry our society forward in this new century?

A transformed school will not look like that brick building set apart from the society it is intended to serve. A transformed school will be an integrated part of the community and its students will be active participants in and contributors to the community. In short, *a transformed school will look more like life.*

A Change in Nature

School right now is as much—or possibly more—about what to do with our children for most of the sixteen to eighteen years that they cannot well survive on their own as it is about truly preparing them for and helping them lead productive and fulfilling lives.

So much of the language of school has more to do with conformance, standardization, and remediation than creativity, opportunity, or self-actualization. The focus of schools needs to shift radically to the latter—but saying this just barely scratches the surface of what needs to happen. The nature of schools is deeply connected with the nature of all of our other major institutions, particularly work and government. A true transformation in the nature of schools can be achieved only if there is transformation in these other areas.

At work, we already see signs of such a transformation. We have long since left the world of the secure, lifelong, nine-to-five job. Most of us now work in the state of flux and insecurity that characterizes our new economy. This is the negative side of the equation, but the positive side is the high degree of flexibility and choice this new world of work can offer to those who embrace it.

While unions and other organizations continue to fight for the rights workers enjoyed under the old economy, most of us have yet to claim our rights to the positive side of the new economy. Many of us do not need to be tied to place anymore to do our work; most of us do not need to be tied to the same rigid schedules that have defined previous work. Everything about our current K–12 education system aligns to the fact that the vast majority of parents have to be in a particular place for a particular period of time each day in order to earn an income. And this constraint has become even more rigid as more and more households require two incomes to make ends meet. Both workers and businesses need to wake up to the new realities. As the possibilities for freeing work from time and place develop, however, so do the possibilities for school.

But this type of shift will not occur until governments wake up and begin to fully support it. A recent Georgetown University Center on Education and the Workforce report argues that governments are too focused on supporting labor from an industry perspective. They are geared toward supporting institutions like, for example, the auto or financial services industries, when—the reports authors suggest—they should be focused on helping individuals pursue occupations.[41] Taking this a step further, government policies should be geared toward helping individuals develop *capabilities* that will be broadly applicable throughout their lives, no matter what their occupation or industry. True support from this perspective requires not simply a change in educational policies, but much deeper rethinking of how we design our cities, how broadband and wireless access should be managed, and what the social safety net really needs to be like for a society that is increasingly made up of de facto "free agents."

A transformed educational system will be a deeply integrated part of our communities and it will be *a place where a lifelong process of capability development begins.*

SIGNALS FROM THE FUTURE

While changes such as running more wires into schools and changing the elements of the curriculum may have a positive impact on our schools, they smack of playing catch-up, of simply trying to keep ourselves in the current global game. But if we expect to be prepared for a future we can hardly foresee, we cannot simply play catch-up. We must think differently. We must leap forward.

A transformation of the magnitude suggested here will not come easily or without pain, but it will likely come faster than any of us imagine. In the coming chapters, we hear the perspectives of individuals who already sense that significant change is afoot, and we take a look at some of the "signposts" that point toward the sort of transformation suggested. In some cases, it will be necessary for us to make sweeping changes across the policies and practices that govern our current educational system. It will also be necessary to make a significant financial investment if we really hope to achieve our educational goals. But there are also smaller steps we can each take to help move us forward. It is a matter of each and all of us making the choice to do so.

KEY POINTS

- Transformation will come whether we want it or not—the forces already at work are simply too powerful. The only real question is whether we lead it or become overwhelmed by it.
- We view transformation as "a change in form, appearance, nature and character" and see changes coming in each of these areas:
  - Form: a shift away from the "box" form that has characterized not just schools themselves, but the entire way we think about schools
  - Appearance: a shift away from schools that look as much like containment areas or prisons as anything else.
  - Nature and character: a shift toward schools that are not separate, isolated entities, but rather vibrant centers of activity fully integrated into their communities.
- The majority of current reform efforts are reactionary and based on playing catch-up. We must think differently.

CHANGE VISIONS

The New Architecture of Learning

Steven Turckes, architect, Recognized Educational Facility Planner (REFP), LEED®AP, is the national director of the K–12 Educational Facilities Group for Perkins+Will, an international award-winning architectural firm specializing in the research-based planning and design of innovative and sustainable educational facilities. His twenty-four-year career has focused on the programming, master planning, and implementation of numerous K–12 projects across the nation and abroad totaling over $1 billon. A strategic thinker about the evolving nature of our global society and economy, he often assists schools navigate change to create agile, responsive, and forward-facing learning environments. Melanie Kahl, K–12 education research knowledge coordinator for Perkins+Will, assisted in this change vision.

Vision for Change: An Educational Architect

There is great responsibility and humility in the tangible act of building. In a rapidly changing world where Facebook could be considered the world's third largest country and anyone with an Internet connection can download Stanford University courses on iTunes (for free), planning something of permanence is downright intimidating. The pressure is heightened in education, an institution that is centered on the cultivation of future minds but is too often stuck in outdated methods of instruction. Yes, building a new school or renovating an existing school is daunting. That is, if you take a moment to think about the stakes.

At the twilight of the twentieth century, the National Center for Education Statistics estimated that the average age of U.S. school buildings was forty-two years, with more than a fourth designed and constructed before 1950[1] for an economy that no longer exists. And, what did the technological world look like in the midcentury? The Polaroid was invented in 1947 and whiteout was invented in 1951, and even though the hard drive (1955), optical fibers (1952), and the floppy disk

---

[1]National Center for Education Statistics (n.d.)

(1952) were invented in the 1950s, computers weren't viewed as home essentials until relatively recently.[2] It is safe to say that these midcentury schools, many of which are still presently in operation, did not take into account the technologies of their day, let alone incorporate a framework for future technologies.

What about the advancements of today and the exponentially evolving tomorrow? We are not just living in a world of new invention; we are living in a completely new culture of possibility. At the time of this writing, YouTube viewership, with two billion views daily, trumps the primetime audiences of ABC, NBC, and CBS by nearly double. What's more striking is that over three quarters of those YouTube users are between ages 13 and 30.[3] This fact alone reveals that the way in which young people consume entertainment, socialize, *and* learn has changed. Parents of youngsters today probably know that if their children want to know "how" to do something, they head to YouTube where in a matter of seconds they will find a video on the subject. What is radically different about these new forms of media? Participation, personalization, creation, immediacy—this new world empowers agency and connection that traditional teacher-directed instruction struggles to compete with and outmoded school buildings handicap.

If we were to decide today to build a new school, to go through the visioning, financing, design, and construction process alone could take three to five, or more, years. The doors would open around 2015 and would close, if past trends are any indication, about 2060. In that time, thousands of students will have passed through the doors of our imagined facility in its lifetime. Extrapolate that further to the approximately two thousand new schools opening in a given year—and millions of students will be learning, developing, and connecting in schools that begin planning in the next twelve months alone.[4]

---

[2]Timeline of historic inventions (n.d.); Pew Research Center (2006). According to the Pew Charitable trusts only 51 percent of surveyed American adults viewed home computers as a necessity in 2006, as compared to 26 percent in 1996 and 4 percent in 1983.

[3]"YouTube facts & figures" (2010); Van Buskirk (2010); Lardinois (2010)

[4]U.S. Department of Education, National Center for Educational Statistics (2008, 2009a)

Suddenly, a corridor lined with classrooms and lockers to teach reading, writing, and arithmetic doesn't seem quite enough. The stakes of designing a learning environment are high; the risks are irrelevance and inflexibility, and restriction for a generation of learners, teachers, and administrators are real. And so the task of *just* "building a schoolhouse" seems woefully inadequate. Yes, building a school is important, real, and intimidating—but mostly, it's exciting. It's exciting because educational architects and planners must be futurists in their own right. It's exciting because it is an opportunity to connect design and learning.

Our Future Framework

Entering this world of creating learning environments for the next century, we must accept two fundamental principles: (1) design matters and (2) planning schools can be a catalyst of change for a community. Stock school plans from a prescribed vision of what school should be are not adequate for diverse communities with evolving needs and goals.

Design

When design is participatory, sustainable, and responsive to the larger world, the impact is remarkable. Sensitive design anticipates needs and inspires behaviors in communities that can promote safety, health, collaboration, creativity, and technological use. Sustainable design can vastly change a building's bottom line and impact on the larger environment, saving financial resources for educational investments and preserving the environment for future generations to enjoy. And finally, good design can enhance educational programs and have the power to inspire and uplift.

Planning

To truly launch schools and communities into the future, we must capitalize on the opportunity to plan collaboratively and build schools that are sensitive to each unique locality. The planning of a school is an opportunity to involve diverse stakeholders from the school, community, and industry and challenge them to envision the future for which they are preparing students and what those students will need to succeed. We see these sessions as inspiring and challenging, as entire communities cross-pollinate and dream together, often for the first time. These visioning sessions turn into concrete discussions of how to shape their school to fit their educational, cultural, and economic goals. Schools born out of this planning are positioned to act as a catalyst for change for a community, fostering the best of practices in sustainability and preparation.

The Architect's Eye: The Future of Educational Environments

Sustainability: Moving Beyond Requirements

At roughly 4.7 percent of the world's population, the United States produces about 20.6 percent of the world's greenhouse gas emissions.[5] As the economies in developing countries such as India and China continue to mature, resources will grow increasingly scarce and their allocation will become increasingly important. Collectively, we simply cannot sustain current rates of consumption. Buildings account for 72 percent of electricity consumption and 39 percent of carbon dioxide emissions in the United States—and school buildings alone are the educational and occupational home to about 20 percent of the population.[6] Schools are ideally poised to act as sentinels for sustainable design for their communities and the next generation of leaders. Fortunately, schools across the United States are jumping on board and adopting the popular Leadership in Energy and Environmental Design (LEED®) certification system sponsored by the U.S. Green Building Council (USGBC).

But the future will require us to go beyond the basics to more holistic design aimed at carbon neutrality, or better yet, regenerative or living buildings. Guidelines and collaboratives are already developing strategies towards these ends and several promising projects have popped up around the world. But what if our educational system were so intrepid as to lead the living building movement? Bringing operational efficiency and sustainable lessons to the hearts of communities and into the everyday lives of 20 percent of Americans (not to mention 100 percent of the future generation) could quite literally begin to change the world—in health, outputs, but moreover, philosophy.

---

[5]Baumert (2005)

[6]U.S. Green Building Council (n.d.)

Connectivity: Embracing Agility and Ubiquity

For schools to launch into the future, they will also need to embrace a holistic view of connectivity—within spaces, amongst diverse collaborators, and with the larger world. It is tempting to think of connectivity and envision the future of education in technical hardware—new gadgets and gizmos on every surface. Not only do the realities of exponential change and tightened budgets render this vision superficial, but a focus solely on *acquiring* hardware misses the mark. We must learn from the intuitive, agile, and connective design of technology, rather than attempt to fit every room to the latest iPod or interactive whiteboard. Our environments need to be integrated, rather than piecemeal, to maximize agility and empower diverse learning modalities. Just like the moment we pick up an iPhone, and we know how to use it, schools need to be designed to "get out of the way" of learning. Environments should be both flexible and responsive, empowering learners by seamlessly transitioning to accommodate the independent virtual scholar, interdisciplinary teams, the traditional lecture, a community forum, and other forms of teaching and learning. Instead of merely trying to fit our schools with the latest digital product from year to year, we must go deeper into cultivating savvy skills in our students and placing them in agile environments that support connected learning.

Just as the boundaries within the school environments should be blurred and flexible, we would be remiss not to consider the blurred boundaries of learning in and out of the school. Students should not have to "power down" mentally and technologically when they walk into class, counting the minutes until they can exchange with a friend overseas on Skype (twenty-first-century pen pals) or see the feedback on their latest homemade guitar project on YouTube. Schools should emulate and encourage informal learning that occurs in the outside world—opening their doors later, bringing communities in, year-round, in true partnerships. Although our tests have not yet developed to capture the value inherent in informal learning and collaborative fluency, it should not stop us from designing schools to honor the connections between school and community.

With a plucky collection of edupreneurs, developers, organizers, and designers working alongside adventurous educators and impatient philanthrocapitalists, our future schools will hopefully evolve from contained classrooms into wired, global studios. Future teachers, an increasingly diverse and now powerful bunch, will act as learner guides, not just instructors, leveraging tools to evaluate and maximize their efficiency. Curriculums will balance a sense of do-it-yourself individualization and vetted best practices—open for change and redefinition. Technology and connection will blur the lines between institutions, as schools tap into the resources of renowned universities and think tanks such as TED for content and inspiration. These globalized schools will be poised to be the center of community learning locally—providing the tangible home for communities, students, and families to learn and act together.

I am leaving the visions of technology, industry, and curriculum in the capable hands of scientists and educators in these pages. From the perspective of an architect, the future of education lies in accepting the power of holistic design and collaborative planning and integrating principles of sustainability and connectivity. The true innovation here is not a specific gadget or technology, but the values placed on holistic, intuitive, and collaborative design that will result in efficient and empowering spaces for whole communities of learners.

Working on the Shift Ed Vision

While we have offered visions for change from various contributors throughout the book, this chapter is devoted specifically to commentary from educators who work in the K–12 system. The four people in this chapter represent many hardworking visionaries at all levels of K–12 education. All of them are working to forge a twenty-first-century educational system that can serve all of society.

There are, of course, many other voices and many other examples we could include here. Knowledge is Power Program (KIPP)[42] schools, numerous charter schools, the Teach for America program,[43] and the many programs recognized by the Classroom of the Future Foundation[44] are just a very few examples of the bright spots already identifiable on the educational landscape. This chapter could be filled with hundreds of intelligent, committed voices. Space and the necessary timelines to publish this book are such that we only include a representative sample of those whose mission is to improve education. The people who share their visions here therefore are only a small sampling of thinkers, practitioners, and visionaries who, every day, commit themselves to forging the new landscape for K–12 education for this new century.

The representatives were all asked to respond to the following question:

> What is your vision for the future of K–12 education? What is your thinking about education from cradle to grave in the future? What are the general and specific ways in which you think K–12 education will need to change in the coming ten, twenty, thirty, or more years for America and the world? Please be forward facing. If there are current practices or models you like in today's world, please use them only as directional signposts to what might be in the future.

JIM REX

Jim Rex, PhD, the sixteenth elected state superintendent of education for the state of South Carolina, is a former college president, high school English teacher, and football coach. During his tenure as state superintendent, South Carolina doubled the number of students enrolled in public charter schools, tripled the number of magnet schools, and became a national leader in a number of innovative choices for parents and students—including single-gender and Montessori schools. A strong advocate for comprehensive reform in public education, he promotes an increased role for "citizen-legislators" in American politics as the needed catalyst for meaningful and lasting change.

Our future educational "systems" will become aligned with what we actually know about human growth and development and, in particular, brain function. Quality prenatal care and childcare, universal early childhood education, along with seamless K–16 alternatives will propel unprecedented knowledge and skill attainment for infants, children, adolescents, and adults.

Long-accepted achievement gaps between disadvantaged and advantaged groups will disappear and, rather than celebrate the occasional individual who *beats the odds*, we will instead have *changed the odds* to the extent that virtually all students will succeed at optimal levels for them personally and for us collectively. America will be the first nation to fully implement this knowledge-based, equitable system with a truly diverse citizenry. That diversity, coupled with our nearly universal educational attainment, will become our global competitive advantage.

As the first nation to effectively act upon the knowledge available about how our species develops and learns, we will begin to transform ourselves in just one generation. Twenty years after the implementation of this new "American development model" we will begin to look very different. For example, we will have stopped building prisons, and begun large-scale demolition; stopped the generational cycles of poverty, and ushered in steadily increasing prosperity for new recipients; dramatically decreased the rates of the chronically unemployed and underemployed, and put into play a dynamic learner-centered and knowledge-based workforce. Perhaps most importantly, we will be producing and electing leaders who truly understand the causal relationships between education, workforce development, economic vitality, and quality of life determinants.

Because America's citizens will equal or outperform the rest of the world, while looking much like the rest of the world (diversity), we will become the model for worldwide human capital development. That model, based upon our unique human capacities and proclivities, will produce unprecedented positive outcomes for us—and the world.

PETER RENWICK

Peter Renwick has been principal of Westfield High School in Westfield, New Jersey for two years. Before that, he was an assistant principal for five years and social studies teacher for ten years at Montclair High School in New Jersey. Prior to becoming a teacher, he was a stockbroker when the stock market crashed in 1987. Since becoming an educator, he has continually crafted his vision for good teaching and he has always stressed the importance of education in our society.

As an educator who has committed his adult life to nurturing and challenging schoolchildren and as an active principal, I have often contemplated a vision of the future of education that would support my philosophy of developing a more life-affirming and constructivist approach to learning. My vision has also been influenced by some of the frustrating limitations I see in our current national educational system. I often feel that our nation's children are not getting the proper education they need to prepare them for the unique challenges of this new century, and many recent studies support my fears. I am certain that we can do better, and that we must do better, if we are to continue to thrive as a nation and world community. Working each day in a high-performing and caring high school does not limit my frustration for the future of all of our children. Recognizing the challenges many students face each day has given me incentive to evaluate how education might be better in the decades to come.

As is the case with any successful leader, the great ideas of others influence my current philosophies and future vision. The concepts of a life- affirming curriculum, igniting a culture of inquiry and imagination, integrative and communal curriculum, and connected and holistic learning have been directly influenced by the work of Stephanie Pace Marshall in her extraordinary book *The Power to Transform: Leadership That Brings Learning and Schooling to Life.* In the future, I believe all educational institutions will better honor our students' innate desire for learning through a more life-affirming process of exploration that

- Instills wonder
- Encourages problem solving
- Constructs meaning and relevance
- Values discovery

By better understanding the ways in which we learn, schools and educators in the future will be appropriately equipped with the knowledge and skills necessary to provide a more generative, integrative, and communal curriculum that makes meaningful connections within a holistic context, while instilling deep thinking in a culture of inquiry and imagination.

I believe education will meet students where they are and help them get to where they want to be with far fewer limitations. As we advance into a global economy and worldwide culture, teaching and learning will move more and more out of the classroom and into the real world. Education will focus on solving problems so that students learn valuable lessons more from meaningful experiences that incorporate past learning and spark new insights. Our schools will center on the discovery of knowledge, fostering of creativity, and development of wisdom in a community setting that involves all constituents and stakeholders of our society, rather than being limited to our current schoolhouse concept.

I also believe that technology will help everyone learn without limits; students of all ages will have access to the information they seek and can use this information in meaningful and practical ways that build knowledge without restrictions, such as time and distance. Today, some other limits of our national education system include age-specific and fragmented curriculum; prescribed classroom instruction; inadequate funding; lessons that do not engage or excite students; instruction that is not meaningful, relevant, or does not lead to effective transfer of knowledge; and a lack of vision for how we, as educators, need to face these challenges and embrace a new vision that honors a child's innate sense of wonder and desire to learn.

Another factor that will have an enormous influence on how people learn will be our continuing advancements in brain research. With a better understanding of how we learn, educators will be better prepared to teach for improved learning and students will be able to build skills in the most effective manner. Clearly, we cannot fully imagine the changes our world will see over the next few decades, as change is occurring so fast already and will only continue exponentially.

However, I do believe that our states of mind and consciousness will change and adapt to new technologies and the new understandings we gain about our universe and ourselves. Quite possibly, we will be able to communicate with anyone we chose at any time about any topic or interest. These opportunities will open up new pathways for learning that we currently cannot fully comprehend, but are nevertheless very exciting to consider. Instant access to information and greater contact with experts will enable future learners to acquire information and new skills at their own pace while allowing those who are disadvantaged in any way to have greater abilities to learn in the most ideal setting as well.

To me, the most exciting possibilities lie in the realm of consciousness; how we interpret and understand our thoughts, emotions, and the way we interact with the world, both internally and externally. Advancements over the last decade point to exciting new ways to communicate, discover, and wonder that come from our new understandings of consciousness. I am confident that the future of education will also include ways to gain a greater connectedness to our world, each other, and ourselves. I believe we will better learn how to manage our social and emotional needs as well as achieve a greater sense of personal satisfaction with our lives and achieve a deeper level of happiness. Once we fully comprehend the full power of the brain, and the mind, our potential for learning and achieving will truly be unlimited.

These are challenging times. Therefore, our vision for education must incorporate advances we have made thus far, embrace opportunities for new technologies, and integrate new insights about how we learn. This approach will move us into a new world where education leads the way and allows us to meet our greatest potential.

JANICE MATTINA

Janice Mattina has been an educator for over forty years. A certified Montessori instructor for over thirty years, she started Center

Montessori School for her own children in 1976 to provide an alterna-
tive education in an environment respectful of the whole child. As a
graduate of the University of South Florida in Tampa, public school
teacher both in California and Florida, reading and math consultant,
parent and teacher instructor in redirecting children's behavior, and
expert on instructing children on conflict resolution, she has devoted her
life to children and helping give them the tools to live happier, more
fulfilled lives. A proud parent of four and grandparent to six children
(five of whom attend the school she founded), in her spare time she
writes poetry about nature and wildlife.

I, too, have a dream about the future of education for the children's sake. My dream is that children, all children, will be
respected as competent learners before we educators try to
teach them anything. I hope that we can realize that the intel-
lectual work children do to teach themselves before they go to
school, while majorly unrecognized, is nothing less than
remarkable. Children are their own best teachers and teach
themselves many skills perfectly before they even enter
school, in fact so perfectly that they never have to review or
reinstruct themselves.

Probably the most difficult work any person does in one's
lifetime is to teach oneself one's native tongue, one's first
foreign language. Yet almost all of us do this by the time we
are three years young without any formal education, without
any lessons from anyone, without homework, tests, reviews,
external motivation, textbooks, grades, or relearning. How
did this happen? We used the powers of our mind to do this.
We did not use our memory, which is a weak power of the
mind and which needs all this support. Schools of the past
built themselves upon the child's weakest power, memory.
Schools of the future will no longer use memory for learning
but will use the powers of the mind that are stronger and
more efficient. These are the powers children all used
as they taught themselves to speak. What this means is
that there is something to be learned from watching children
learn.

So how would schools that respect children as capable learners look in the future? First of all, they would look interesting to children or students who would use them. They would be places where children—students—want to be, work, and spend time. Schools in this ideal future will also look physically different than they do today and different from each other. Educators here take great care to create appealing classrooms that are kept clean, organized, and orderly by all cooperating together to maintain them. Each school itself and its environment as well as its curriculum is created for the particular family age group that will use it. Children are grouped by family age groups based on three-year planes of development (first identified by Maria Montessori and later supported by others). Primary school would be ages 3 to 6, elementary would be ages 6 to 9, and ages 9 to 12. Middle school would be ages 12 to 15. High school would be ages 15 to 18, and higher education would be ages 18 to 21 and ages 21 to 24.

Each classroom in this vision is equipped with the kinds of curricular materials the particular age group needs based on scientific information regarding children's abilities to abstract concepts. For example, for children ages 4 through 12, mathematics is taught using all sorts of concrete materials for learning the operations (plus, minus, multiplication, and division) with emphasis on developing the mathematical mind through a growing awareness of how numbers function rather than learning to rely upon memorizing for knowing. As children gain the ability to abstract math concepts, they elect to begin to work without materials and instead work abstractly. Textbooks would be obsolete and children instead use the computer to attain up-to-date information, read books, find written work assignments, and access all sorts of electronic information.

As another example of how this looks, middle school students would have activities that enable them to make contributions to society and to their own group as a whole. For instance, middle school students operate school businesses like running the school's hot lunch program. The money earned is used to support the group taking overnight adventurous field trips.

This also satisfies another need of this age group—the need to feel important and valued by the adult community. Middle school itself no longer operates or looks like a high school, but is a smaller community with teachers who are also able to act as nurturing mentors for the students. Some academic learning is replaced with outside classroom experiences like field trips, community service, and career internships.

Classrooms themselves would be organized so as to encourage children to feel comfortable being there and working. Children are given freedoms within the classrooms so as to show respect for them as learners, who are already able to learn, concentrate, focus, work, and accomplish. Different kinds of seating arrangements are available from small group gatherings to individual workspaces. Children are permitted to select where they want to work and what work they want to do first. Children are permitted to work individually or with partners and to speak quietly and respectfully to each other as they work.

The curriculum would be established to accommodate the interests of the age of the student. Children move through this curriculum as they master the skills, some taking and needing more time for certain lessons and others needing and taking less time. The teacher presents lessons either individually or to small groups of children. The teacher comes to the presentation with many lessons in mind and begins with one. As the lesson is presented the teacher enters into a dance with the child where the child feeds back to the teacher and the teacher interprets this feedback and lets it guide the next phase of the lesson. This way each lesson becomes individualized to the student as it happens. It is not one that is presented the same for every child but rather one that is specially presented with the child's learning in mind as the lesson progresses.

The child takes an active part in her own learning and can identify when and with what she needs help. She gets to be a responsible learner at school just as she was before she came to school. Testing is not required because the teacher is now in such close contact with every child as a learner that he doesn't need to test to find out what the student knows. Instead the teacher uses observations of the child and his own interpretation of the child's feedback during the lessons to understand what the child knows. Grading also is not used. Schools become competency based, places where children learn because the work presented is interesting to them, places where children learn because the lessons accommodate them and their abilities to learn, places where the next lesson rides on the back of the previous lesson, and places where children are not afraid to make mistakes. Mistakes are now viewed as feedback given honestly and freely from the child to the teacher.

The paradigm has changed so that now teachers are interested and curious about children learning and are willing to subordinate their lessons to the child's learning. In the future, when children don't learn, the teacher will then ask herself the question, "What can I do so that this child learns?" instead of asking what is wrong with the child. Gone are the alphabet soup descriptions of children's inabilities to learn because the science of education has taught us all that children were able to learn something on their own before they came to school, which was harder than any of our lessons. If they did that, then they can teach themselves our lessons. The teacher's job is to be interesting, not boring, to present something for which the child shows an interest, knowing that all children are curious and want to learn.

When public education was institutionalized, its goal was to produce responsible citizens who could maintain a free, democratic country. That notion will be expanded in the future to include producing members of society who can solve problems with other countries in a peaceful manner to maintain world peace. To that end, schools for the future will incorporate a system of discipline that follows Alfred Adler's ideas. Children will create their own peaceful classrooms. They will democratically decide, by voting, what class rules they want. They will learn to solve interpersonal problems with each other by learning how to express their feelings verbally to each other. Problems will be solved by children negotiating to do deeds of kindness to each other as a means of correcting deeds of unkindness or disrespect. Children will no longer be manipulated by rewards or punishments but will learn to make socially appropriate decisions through dialogue with each other. Children will be respected and will have their social needs of feeling important, having power, and being a part of the group met. Mutual respect between children and adults will be practiced at all schools.

In the future, children will be seen as human beings in formation. They will be viewed as children and not adults until the age of maturity, twenty-one. They will be loved and nurtured and respected. The schools of the future will be heavily funded both at the state and federal levels because our society will finally value children for what they are, the gifts for our future.

KAREN WOODWARD

Karen Woodward, PhD, has been a superintendent for twenty-six years. Since 2000, she has served as superintendent of Lexington County School District One in Lexington, South Carolina. She was named one of four finalists for National Superintendent of the Year and one of the Top Ten Tech Savvy Superintendents in the nation. She has also received the South Carolina Commission on Women's Pioneer Award, South Carolina Business Woman of the Year Award, the Governor's Educational Champion of the Year Award, and both the South Carolina School Boards Association's and the South Carolina Association of School Administrators' Superintendent of the Year awards. Described as a visionary who gets things done, her career has focused on advocacy for children and public service.

Public Education: What Is Our Vision of the Twenty-First-Century Graduate?

We are now ten years into the twenty-first-century and our world is transforming.

In this period of history, we will experience a world shaped by breakneck change driven in large part by the electronic revolution that is shrinking our world and reorganizing all that is familiar to us.

An increasingly global orientation characterizes this change, along with pervasive access to information and knowledge, continuous communication and collaboration, and electronic connectedness in ways never experienced.

Knowledge and the ability to innovate and create have become the commodities that are valued and that produce wealth.

All of this gives rise to relentless global and local *stresses* affecting all of us economically, socially, politically, culturally, and personally. Our world is significantly more complex.

This complex, electronic, global, competitive twenty-first century gives rise to the need for and capability of individuals to be self-directed.

Nationally, the history of public education as the foundation of economic prosperity and democratic freedom, and individually, the route to social mobility bettering the lives of many, is well documented. Public schools must remain the center of the community in the future as in the past. They may look differently and act differently, but they must continue to serve as the place where people come together to learn and practice democracy and citizenship. If we fail to provide this opportunity in the future, we fail our children and our country. The Shift Age will require sophisticated thinking for sound decision making as twenty-first-century leaders and citizens.

The risks that public education faces if we do not respond to—and more importantly do not anticipate—those changes is first, to miseducate our students for the twentieth century instead as graduates for the twenty-first century and second, to jeopardize the United States as a global leader in democracy and the innovative engine necessary for economic viability.

And so, we must rethink:

- What does a successful graduate in the twenty-first century look like?

- How must the public education system be transformed to prepare that new graduate, and to provide what America and our democracy need for the twenty-first century?

What Does the Twenty-First-Century Graduate Look Like?

Twenty-first-century graduates are a new generation of leaders and global citizens who are self-directed, creative, collaborative, caring, and multilingual. They are individuals who will flourish in a global, competitive twenty-first century.

Our graduates must be confident in academics, sophisticated in learning, accomplished in twenty-first-century skills, global in orientation, and prepared as leaders and citizens of our twenty-first-century democracy.

The top ten in-demand jobs in 2010 did not exist in 2004. Half of what students starting a four-year degree in technical areas now learn in the first year of study will be outdated by their third year of study. The amount of new technical information doubles every year.

This new century, once again, needs *graduates who are self-directed, collaborative, creative, caring, and multilingual.* We need graduates who are confident in academics, sophisticated in learning, accomplished in twenty-first-century skills, global in orientation, and prepared as leaders and citizens of our twenty-first-century democracy.

More specifically our graduates must

- Have deep learning in liberal arts and the areas of STEM.
- Acquire sophisticated skills of learning (e.g., analyze, synthesize, evaluate, problem solve, innovate, and continue to learn).
- Understand leadership and apply leadership skills throughout their lives.
- Understand the importance of civil discourse, the requirements of a democracy, and good citizenship.

- Be able to communicate in a media-saturated society.
- Understand the power of collaboration and master collaborative skills.
- Use and manage electronic tools.
- Have a global orientation, understand other cultures, and be multilingual.
- Have integrity and sensitivity, be astute in identifying the needs of others, and care about those needs.
- Grasp the importance of personal fulfillment, the joy of being, and behaviors that affect these states.

How Will Public Education Shift to Develop the Twenty-First-Century Graduate? What Is Our Vision of Schooling?

The development of twenty-first-century graduates occurs with the vision of schooling shifting to the vision of learning. The major forces of the Shift Age and a broader view of our "customers" affects this change.

The most critical shift for public education is the shift of focus from schooling and teaching to *learning* and from students to community learners:

- Shift to thinking about *learning experiences, not education system.* Today people want to experience, to participate, and to be engaged. They look for personalized experiences that are unique, productive, motivating, enjoyable, and meaningful.
- Shift to a *broader learning customer.* The entire community needs flexible, quick, easy access to continuous learning; opportunities to develop and participate as community citizens; and encouragement for collaboration and participation.
- Shift to *continual learning throughout life* (cradle-to-grave learning). Although learning is organic and happens naturally through the times of daily living, some learning must be intentional. Our graduates must be equipped to continue intentional learning throughout life for both personal and professional reasons.

Vision of Learning and the
Learning System in the Future

In general, the future character of education will be a fluid and flexible system of experiences created, organized, and carried out to meet the learning needs of preK–G12 students as well as community citizens. Here are twelve key components to fulfill this transformed system:

1. *Learning (schooling) will become more participant driven, and give pervasive access to information to everyone, along with numerous and optional systems for education and the power of individual choice.*

2. *Learning will shift from thinking about programs and place to thinking about a selection of highly effective, engaging, individually focused learning experiences.* These experiences provide the skills, content knowledge, and global understanding demanded by the times and by those we serve. These experiences will be available anytime, anywhere.

3. *Ultimately, the learning system (districts and schools) will become a part of a network of learning experiences around the world.* The learning system will facilitate access to learning experiences and codify learning accomplishments and certifications ("diploma" or performance standard).

Within this system, each learner will maintain a lifelong dossier of educational and learning accomplishments and attainments including certifications, particular expertise, various learning and work experiences, travel, community action, citizenship responsibilities, and so forth.

4. *Reorganizing roles, relationships, and staffing patterns will emphasize collaborative teams.* Teams will consist of highly trained learning specialists, brain-research practitioners, and other interdisciplinary specialists diagnosing and designing learning. A cadre of various community-related systems will convene on learning and barriers to learning.

The role of teachers and administrators will shift to a focus on serving learning as learning collaborators: creators of sophisticated learning experiences, expert resources in collaborative commons and labs for creative study, diagnosticians and providers of individual assistance for students with learning difficulties, and providers of structured learning experiences and courseware development. The various roles, periods of employment, and work time of learning personnel will be flexible and will modify according to need.

5. *There will be few boundaries of time, space, and place.* Place will be progressively unimportant and time more flexible and personalized. Learning will be cradle to grave, twenty-four hours a day and seven days a week. A hybrid of face-to-face, online, experiential strategies will be used. This will be realized according to the age, learning need, interest, and maturity of learners.

6. *The organization of learning will cease to be around age, grade levels, day, or year.* Organization will instead be according to individual learning goals, units of learning, and assessment for competency. Early childhood learning will begin prebirth for parents and at birth for children, and will be available in the community learning facility and throughout the community both face-to-face and electronically.

7. *Content of core learning experiences will include deep academic content in the liberal arts, the sciences, and world languages.* Experiences designed to study and solve global policy issues such as energy, sustainability, international relations, and economics will be included. Twenty-first-century skills (critical thinking and problem solving, creativity and innovation, research and information fluency, and collaboration and communication) will frame this study. Citizenship and leadership will be interwoven into all learning.

8. *Learning, both product and experienced based, will be certified based on competency and credentials requirements.* Seat time as a method of certification will disappear. Electronic tools will reshape the look and feel of learning and learning management. Personal electronic devices will be standard.

Specialty devices will assist in overcoming deficiencies that interfere with learning (medical devices, brain wave based, etc.). Devices will allow actual "experiencing."

9. *Students will gradually assume responsibility for their learning and the structure of their learning.* They will progressively create their own schedule for learning and system of learning experiences, create and independently access their own content and learning material, and manage their own learning process in collaboration with learning facilitators. They will choose the location of the learning experiences from a structured place of learning to the community, workplace, travel, Internet, courseware, or other preferred medium.

Teachers and students will use twenty-first-century learning tools (laptops, iPads, MP3, teleconferencing, video conferencing, portfolio systems) in their business of learning, increasing flexibility and mobility, and providing for efficient work habits (file sharing, drop boxes, webbing, brainstorming, collaborating and communicating, data analysis, simulations and modeling, organizing and managing information). Technology proficiency and digital citizenship literacy thus will be central to learning experiences.

10. *Community learning facilities will become the community place for learning and collaboration and provide for community convening and exercise of citizenship skills.* At the learning center for the community, citizens will acquire new knowledge and skills, create productions, access information, learn new languages, and receive technology training and other learning experiences needed and desired throughout life. Access to health and social services and other services will be available. Social and entertainment activities will be available.

11. *Physical structures will be designed and used to accomplish particular learning goals, to provide places of collaboration and creative synergy, and to support community convening.* The physical structures (schools) will be flexible, open, accessible, collaborative, and sustainable. They will consist of a variety of spaces such as collaborative commons, innovation labs, creative

participatory space, electronic tools, structured setting for certain learning, and indoor-outdoor learning spaces. The structures will be warm and inviting with a feels-like-home atmosphere including places to relax. They will engage families and community and indeed be the center of the community.

12. *Much learning will occur outside physical structures: online, extended learning into the community, and global and local settings.* Learning services will be provided throughout the community in an attempt to reduce barriers to learning and open access to learning services in coordination with community agencies.

Some of the preceding thoughts about the future are already happening in spots across the country and in our district. Others may be realized well beyond this decade. *The real challenge is going to scale.* Every child, and every community, deserves to have access to quality twenty-first-century learning in quality twenty-first-century facilities.

KEY POINTS

At all levels of K–12 education in America there are hardworking, committed people. Every day, a vision of the educational system's transformation drives these individuals.

7

Ask the Right Questions

Live your questions now, and perhaps even without knowing it, you will live along some distant day into your answers.

—Rainer Maria Rilke

We have taken a look back at the history and the current landscape of K–12 education. We have looked at the new age and century we have entered. We have looked at the different generations and discussed the different ways in which they have impacted or may impact education. We have expressed our belief that nothing less than transformation of education will suffice. In this chapter, we begin the process of transformation by letting go of all that exists and suggest the questions that need to be addressed to begin anew.

There are many questions that can be asked. There are many categories of questions. Offered here are both high-level categories and a number of specific questions that address how to create a vibrant future for K–12 education. This is by no means an exhaustive list. It is intended purely as a start, as at the beginning of the questioning everything must move the process of educational transformation forward. We hope that anyone involved in or connected to education in any way thinks about these questions, thinks about how to answer them, and—most important—does so without legacy thinking, old baggage, or strongly held points of view.

As the renowned and revered Buddhist monk Thich Nhat Hanh said regarding our tendency to hold onto points of view even when they do not serve us well, "Attachment to views is the greatest impediment to the spiritual path." While these words pertain to a spiritual journey, they also offer a powerful message for those seeking to create a new future for education. Simply put, we cannot afford to hold onto views grounded in the past if we want to see the future clearly. When you read the questions that follow, if you feel resistance to any of them, look inward to see what view you hold that is causing this resistance. If you think you have the immediate answer to any of these questions, pause and reflect on what it is from your past experience that allows you to be so certain. If you have not thought about some of these questions—good. This chapter intends to provoke all to really rethink what the future of K–12 education will be.

The questions are grouped into the following categories, which, though not exhaustive, should help organize the process of transformational thinking:

- Technology and connectivity
- Calendar and operations
- Curriculum
- Learning and the brain
- Infrastructure and the physical plant

TECHNOLOGY AND CONNECTIVITY

If we had written this book thirty years ago, we would have asked what role computers would play in education and the classroom. Fifteen years ago, we would have asked how to deal with the coming reality that middle school and high school students will have handheld devices that would instantly connect them with people and knowledge worldwide. Many people would have read those questions with incredulity.

Global Connectivity

The Accelerating Electronic Connectedness of the Shift Age has resulted in a true global electronic village that is connected with few limits to time, distance, or place. That is the world in which we live. This connectivity will only increase at rates and in forms that will be truly astounding. Global connectivity is no longer just a means of connecting, of obtaining information: it is now environmental. We don't just use connectivity: we live *in* it.

Questions

- How much of this connectivity should be brought into the classroom—and is the traditional classroom even the right approach in such a highly connected world?
- How much freedom should students be given in deciding when, where, and how they connect to learn?
- How will living in this environment of connectivity isolate or integrate the school and the classroom?
- How do we balance the two realities we now live in, the physical reality and the screen reality? Are there limits to connectivity that we should attempt to impose upon ourselves?
- How much online coursework is desirable at each level of education, and what counts as coursework?
- What are the skills needed to build and maintain knowledge in social networks, and how do we best teach them?
- How do we ensure that all children have access to the full range of connective technologies and are taught the skills necessary to use them effectively and judiciously?
- How can we most effectively leverage game-based learning approaches within networks to support effective learning?

- How do we help parents better understand the opportunities and challenges a connected world brings—and how these may impact their children?
- What are our responsibilities as connected, global citizens, and how do we balance them with our responsibilities as citizens of nation-states and local communities?

Intelligent Search and Artificial Intelligence

Web search a decade ago was essentially "dumb." The results received from searching a specific phrase or term were determined more than anything else by the tags that were appended to a specific web page by its authors. Google changed this situation dramatically by introducing algorithms that relied on how popular and, by extension, valuable all the other searchers on the web considered a particular resource. This constituted a sort of collective intelligence that is becoming even more powerful as we devise ways for computers to understand not just the raw definitions of words on a page but their semantics—in other words, the ways in which they fit together to create meaning. Simultaneously—and in part building off of these advances in search technologies—we continue to make progress in the area of artificial intelligence, the ability for nonbiological entities like computers to make productive decisions based upon perceptions of information and other environmental cues. The impact these advances may ultimately have upon learning and our understanding of concepts like knowledge and intelligence seems certain to be enormous. We are already seeing our students' widespread adoption of current search technologies. As the tools that support our ways of knowing advance dramatically, we must be as prepared as possible for the impact on education.

Questions

- What constitutes *knowledge* when all information is connected and machines can act with intelligence in retrieving it?

- How should intelligent search be integrated into the classroom and homework?
- How should intelligent search redefine the word *research?*
- How can intelligent search accelerate learning?
- How should intelligent search alter the curriculum?
- How do we help students protect themselves to the greatest extent possible against any opportunities that may exist for "gaming" these new systems of intelligence?
- Even given the tremendous advances in search, how can individuals manage vast quantities of information in ways that are meaningful and productive?
- How will the growth of artificial intelligence in our connective technologies change education, research, and the classroom?
- As machines know more and more, what do humans most need to know?
- It is predicted that there will be real time, voice recognition, language translation available on laptops and handheld devices by 2014. How do we, or do we need to, teach languages?

Brain Wave Computer Interface

We are now at the early, foundational stage of brain wave interfaces—devices that allow direct communication between the human brain and computers—as a viable mass product. Within a decade it is likely that video gamers will no longer use handheld controllers but will wear head gear that will map their brain waves so that games will be played using the brain waves. This may sound as though it is science fiction but it is here now and will become increasingly affordable and universal.

Questions

- How do we teach students in the classroom in 2020 when they are brain wave interfacing with their computers at home?

- How might brain wave technology accelerate the learning process and affect self-directed learning?
- As brain-computer interfaces become a part of how students engage in educational activities, what are the implications for how we measure a student's performance? Where does the human learner end and the machine begin?
- What are the ethical implications of augmented intelligence, and how do we best teach these to our students?

We all understand that technology has dramatically affected education at all levels. The preceding questions point to the reality that the technological impact on learning, on all levels of education, has only just begun and we have entered a truly transformative time.

CALENDAR AND OPERATIONS

As we and many others have argued, we operate our schools according to an agrarian calendar and with methods born out of the Industrial Age. These approaches are fundamentally out of sync with the Shift Age and the twenty-first century, but collectively we have done little to question their value, much less to make meaningful changes to them. We are long past the point at which we need to ask the hard questions and then act appropriately on the answers.

Questions

- What is the ideal school year—and is the concept of a school year even compatible with the requirements of a postindustrial, postinformation world?
- Is the current definition of summer vacation still valid? What are the alternatives?
- What is the ideal school day at each level of education?
- What grade levels should we have and are they related to age? Is the traditional concept of grade levels even of value any longer?

- How long should a class period last at each level of education, and according to what criteria?
- How do we best establish a flow of time and operations in our schools that meets the needs of an increasingly diverse set of stakeholders and accommodates individual student needs as well as possible?

CURRICULUM

Our notions of curriculum, of what we regard as the actual substance of education, is perhaps more anchored in the past than any other aspect of education. The mindset around what our students learn and how they learn mirrors a factory model: a five-year-old enters the educational assembly line in kindergarten and—assuming we don't lose him along the way—exits as an eighteen-year-old high school graduate filled with knowledge from the past. As if we are building cars on a Detroit assembly line, we assume that we can increase difficulty and layer on new knowledge to each child in a linear, sequential fashion over the years. We all know human beings don't work that way, and yet we persist in our folly. To the extent that we debate curriculum, the arguments tend to be rooted in whether it is more important to teach specific content or broader learning skills—the "what" of education. Thus, we currently have the core-knowledge camp pitted against the twenty-first-century skills camp. Serious questioning of the "how"—with the understanding that debating curriculum within the context of outdated institutions is of little value—receives less attention. We must ask equally serious questions about both what and how if we are to transform education.

Questions

- Does the idea of a common, standardized curriculum make sense in a hyperconnected, rapidly changing world? If so, what are the critical points of commonality and standardization and what are the ways in which it makes sense to "customize" education to the needs of individual learners?

- How do we better teach skills that we already know are essential in our rapidly changing world, like empathy, creativity, and the ability to work collaboratively to solve complex problems?
- How do we best help teachers determine the right balance between teaching content and teaching skills?
- What amount of the curriculum of the present and past must be maintained?
- Can we accelerate the learning of what we chose to keep from this legacy curriculum?
- Can the curriculum that a student needs most be taught effectively within a traditional classroom setting?
- How much of the curriculum can and should be online?
- How do we make the most effective uses of open educational resources and technologies as part of our approach to curriculum development and management?
- What are the essential qualities needed to be a productive, happy member of human society in the next fifty years?
- How do we educate our young to prepare them for the occupations that do not yet exist but will dominate their adult lives?
- How will the United States define its role in the coming second stage of the global economy that will take form in the next ten years? If, for example, we view leadership in innovation as critical, then how do we prepare our children for an innovation society?
- Does education change by country as each country finds its place in a more integrated, connected, and complementary global economy?

LEARNING AND THE BRAIN

Science is now just beginning to delve deeply into all the aspects of the brain. The rapidly developing world of brain science, with ever faster and detailed electronic imaging, is opening up the understanding of how our brains work to an unprecedented degree. How can this science, and the almost daily insights into the working of the brain, be used to redefine education?

We have learned more about how the brain works in the past few decades than in all the time before. We are learning more each year about the magnificence of the human brain than we learned in decades during the last century. This knowledge, these discoveries *must* be brought into the conversation regarding the future of K–12 education. We have an educational system largely developed prior to the current cascading insights of brain science.

Questions

- What do we now know about the brain that is in conflict with past educational beliefs and practices?
- How can we apply the growing knowledge of how the brain develops in childhood and adolescence to alter the stages or sequences of education?
- How can this growing understanding of the brain best enable us to use the technologies that are present today and new ones that will come into existence in the coming decades?
- How can our knowledge that every brain is wired differently help us to move toward individual customization of education rather than the standardization that exists today?

INFRASTRUCTURE AND THE PHYSICAL PLANT

We have written about how all of education seems to be in various boxes. We have suggested that the school buildings in our society often resemble jails—or factories—in their forbidding isolation and institutionalization. We currently segregate our young from society and keep them largely in a state of containment until they can break free in their late teenage years. This must change.

Questions

- If not a boxlike classroom, then what?
- What is the future of the library when a seven-year-old first grader can be handed an e-reader that has on it the 3,500 books she might need through high school or college?
- How can the buildings where we teach our young be more integrated into society?
- What does the school building of the twenty-first century look like? What are its attributes?
- Is "the school" only—or even *mostly*—a physical place?
- How should the buildings of K–12 education be integrated into the coming new transportation, energy, and communications infrastructures of this century?
- How do we help government officials, school boards, architects, builders, and other key decision makers better understand the opportunities and challenges of transformation?

ANSWERING THE QUESTIONS

As stated previously, the reason to ask all these questions is to ensure that those of us committed to transforming K–12 education fully integrate twenty-first-century reality into the education of our children. Asking these questions should serve as a catalyst for creative and innovative brainstorming. Our hope is that this brainstorming will lead to entirely new, fresh, innovative, and future-facing educational realities.

We are hardly the first people to raise some of these questions, nor do not believe we have the answers to all of the questions we raise or to the many others that need to be asked. Even if we did have all of the answers, we would hesitate to provide them, for the process of arriving at the answers is as important as the answers themselves. It must be a collaborative effort shared by people with deep expertise, newcomers with fresh ideas, and all other interested stakeholders. We must create and *own* the change together. As our part in that process, we suggest the general direction to take for each of the categories. We leave the specific answers for the larger collective effort of those who agree that transformation is the process we must now begin.

Technology and Connectivity

Of all the categories, this one is subject to the fastest rate of innovation and change. Even the few classrooms that were technologically state of the art ten years ago are now out of date. It is almost impossible to predict the state of technology and connectivity in 2030, let alone 2050. But we must attempt to set a direction or else be swept along by whatever the future brings.

The starting point is to accept our current reality. We must accept the reality that soon every child over the age of twelve (and perhaps younger) will have a handheld communication device. Accept that universal wireless connectivity will be a part of society and education. Accept that technology is moving us toward interacting directly with each other and with the world around us by using our brain waves and thoughts, and that learning is no longer about mastering a body of factual knowledge that can be much more easily accessed using sophisticated search tools. Technology has become one of the most pervasive and powerful elements of human society today and it must be fully used in education. This inevitably means taking steps that will initially not feel comfortable to many stakeholders—like dramatically reducing the barriers many schools have erected between children and the Internet.

Since the passage of the Children's Internet Protection Act (CIPA) in 2000, schools that wish to receive federal E-rate funding, which provides for affordable telecommunications and Internet access, must implement policies and safeguards for Internet use. Whether as a result of state and local policy or simply to avoid the issues the administrators feel may come with allowing greater access, many schools go much further than CIPA requires in filtering and blocking Internet access. We do, of course, want to ensure that our children are as safe online as possible, but the effectiveness of blocking and filtering in achieving this aim is questionable at best. As numerous critics have argued, even the most effective software often blocks a significant amount of useful content. And our children, adept as they are with technology, often find ways around the software anyway. A simple Google search on "Internet filtering software" or similar terms produces any number of resources to help "hack" the way around the barriers that schools implement.

Much more important than the technical issues with blocking and filtering are the lost educational opportunities. As adults, our children will have to know how to use the wide range of technologies now available as well as the new ones that are likely to come available in the coming years. There is no better time to teach them how to use the technology effectively than during their school years, but we can hardly hope to do this successfully if we limit access to the key tools. As the technology director for a school district that has significantly relaxed its filtering approach puts it, "I don't see how you can teach kids 21st-century values if you're not teaching them digital citizenship and appropriate ways of sharing and using everything that's available on the Web."[45] And we should not assume that simply because our children are digital natives that they have the right skill sets to make effective use of the technologies at which they are so adept. A number of studies suggest that *media literacy* is a skill that the young lack and must be taught.[46]

This skill set is important not only with respect to the future. Given continually tight budget environments as well as a growing need for schools to meet diverse curricula needs—for example, to make available Mandarin Chinese or other languages that have not traditionally been taught in U.S. schools—it is inevitable that more of K–12 education will move online. Locking down these experiences so that students cannot take advantage of the full range of what the web has to offer is not only impractical, it is pedagogically undesirable.

The bottom line is that technology cannot be resisted, only embraced. Technology speeds up the acquisition of knowledge, enhances and expands the ability to interact and collaborate, and will continue to eliminate place and time as limitations on education. But we must prepare our children effectively for these benefits, and that starts with immediately bringing technology fully into our current educational environments.

Calendar and Operations

The rhythms of the world have changed dramatically in the last fifty years, far more than those in education. The world is now 24/7/52, but education is not. That has to change. The first step is to decide that standardized school years and school days for all ages at all stages of the K–12 educational process are no longer valid, assuming they ever were. They do not align with the current world of work—as they did in the agricultural and factory days—and they do not serve our students well.

The entire concept of a three-month summer vacation, for example, needs to be fully rethought. This long break is a clear holdover from the agricultural era, and one that makes no sense in the current age. What other area of society or future-facing industry shuts down for 25 percent of the year? And why would we assume that learning essentially stops for three months out of the year, as the break from the classroom implies? As advocates of a longer school year, including U.S. Secretary of Education Arne Duncan,[47] have argued, students in other countries—ones that are outperforming us in many areas of education—spend more time in school. Additionally, there is evidence that summer vacation contributes to under-privileged kids falling behind their more affluent peers. While middle- and upper-class children often attend summer camps, take family vacations, and participate in various types of summer enrichment programs, many poorer kids spend their time simply hanging out or watching TV. And regardless of socio-economic factors, the three-month summer gap can often lead to kids forgetting a significant amount of what they learned during the school year.[48]

Of course, there is no point in forcing kids to spend more time in schools that are underperforming or that serve as little more than a containment area. The elimination of the traditional summer vacation period would need to accompany the other changes we advocate in this chapter and throughout this book including, most important, tighter integration of schools into communities. Moreover, vacation should not be eliminated entirely, but rather distributed into breaks throughout the year, as many schools that have adopted year-round calendars have already done. Shorter, distributed periods would have numerous advantages. From a pedagogical standpoint, they provide a break from study that may support the consolidation of learning while not allowing a large enough gap for significant forgetting. From a resource standpoint, it would be more manageable for schools and other organizations to provide enrichment programs and other opportunities over shorter time periods—time periods that are short enough that they could also be much more attractive to community volunteers. From the standpoint of working households, there would no longer be the issue of how to handle a very large gap of time that often requires significant expenditure, unpaid time away from work, or both.

These are just a few of the potential advantages. No doubt you can think of many more. And as you think about the potential for moving to year-round schooling, we encourage you to think about other aspects of the school calendar and operations. Summer, for example, has not only been a traditional time for vacation, it has also represented the dividing line between one grade and the next. But what if grades were eliminated as well? Can the factory concept of matriculating through twelve grades that worked for 1910 really still be relevant today? We all know that the children who comprise any given grade level in a school usually vary widely in their actual capabilities, levels of achievement, and most important, the ways and pace at which they learn. Many children do not perform at the level we would expect them to for a given grade level while others vastly exceed our expectations. Like standardized testing, we rely on the attainment of higher grade levels throughout a child's education as an assurance that "progress" is being made. But as with standardized testing, we deceive ourselves as often as not.

What if we were to abolish grades entirely and instead work each student to help her advance according to her own abilities and skill level? As John Covington, superintendent of the Kansas City school system puts it,

> The current system of public education in this country is not working. It's an outdated, industrial, agrarian kind of model that lends itself to still allowing students to progress through school based on the amount of time they sit in a chair rather than whether or not they have truly mastered the competencies and skills.[49]

Kansas City follows the example of a number of school systems in implementing an approach that groups students according to ability rather than traditional grade levels. We believe some form of a no-grade-level system is what is needed for the future. Along with this shift, we believe it will be necessary to reexamine what the typical school day is like for each student. Why should the school day or school year of an eight-year-old, for example, even remotely resemble that of a sixteen-year-old?

None of these changes will be easy, of course. They require significant community buy-in and education of key stakeholders like parents, teachers, and administrators. But we need to start the work now to bring education more in line with the rhythms of the rest of the world.

Curriculum

As suggested, curriculum is easily the thorniest and most politicized area of potential educational transformation. Since the rise of progressive educational approaches in the middle of the twentieth century, the discussion has been reduced to an overemphasis on content on the one hand and learning process and skills on the other. Such polarization is senseless and detracts from finding replicable, effective ways to implement curricula with an appropriate focus on both content *and* skills. Of course learning must focus on *something*, and it makes sense for there to be a well-articulated set of standards along the lines of what Common Core State Standards Initiative has defined, an effort the National Governors Association Center for Best Practices and the Council of Chief State School Officers (http://www.corestandards.org/) lead and coordinate. But these should be treated as framework, as a valuable tool that schools and teachers can reference in offering curricula that are shaped to the needs of their student populations and individual learners. Tying a rigid, fixed set of content to them—as some would advocate—seems almost certain to perpetuate the current obsession with standardized measurement, if only in a somewhat different form. In a much more isolated world, this approach may have worked, but in a world where content proliferates at an exponential rate and the borders between nations and cultures grow more blurry daily, there is no way anyone can claim to know a set of core content that best meets the future needs of our students.

At the same time, criticism from supporters of core knowledge that supposedly twenty-first-century skills like critical thinking, teamwork, and problem solving are nothing new is correct to an extent. Successful people have always needed most of the skills that are often touted now as the path to curing our educational ills. But all hype aside, the broad and collective urgency for mastering these skills has never been higher. As we have argued throughout this book, the context in which those skills must be applied and the speed with which that context is changing is simply unparalleled in history. The environment in which most individuals had the opportunity to live, work, and raise children in the past was vastly more proscribed geographically, culturally, and in any number of other ways. The sheer change in the *scale* and *degree* to which key learning skills are now required amounts to a change in *kind*. There is simply no way that students will be prepared for the job and life demands of the future—demands we cannot even remotely foresee at this point—without exceptional facility in thinking processes that are tightly tied to the wide range of technologies that are and will be available. We have little doubt that these skills can only be developed in the context of a content-rich curriculum, but it is also clear that terms like creativity, problem solving, teamwork, and other buzzwords have taken on a whole new meaning in our hyperconnected, information-overloaded world.

The real issue with curriculum has less to do with the specifics of the content or the particular skill sets to be taught and more to do with how we support learning experiences that combine the two effectively. Nearly everything we currently know about effective childhood learning points to smaller classes and more individual attention; toward group and project-based work; toward deep involvement of those who care most about the children, most importantly parents and grandparents. At the same time, nearly everything about our legacy, factory-modeled school systems as well as the constraints of the Industrial Age work schedules prevents us from pursuing these strategies even if we were to muster—as we so far have not—the collective will to fund them properly. This stalemate takes us back to one of the key reasons we have argued in this book not simply for reform but for total transformation: the focus on content and skills in the debate over curriculum is anchored in—and keeps us anchored in—the past. Curriculum cannot and will not change, and the issues that surround it will not be resolved, without the sort of transformation we advocate.

Learning and the Brain

John Medina writes in *Brain Rules: 12 Principles for Surviving and Thriving at Work, Home, and School* that "our schools are designed so that most real learning has to occur at home. This would be funny if it weren't so harmful. Blame it on the fact that brain scientists rarely have a conversation with teachers and business professionals, education majors and accountants, superintendents and CEOs. Unless you have the *Journal of Neuroscience* sitting on your coffee table, you're out of the loop."[50] We may not need to go so far as subscribing every teacher, parent, and administrator to the *Journal of Neuroscience,* but Medina's point is well taken: the amount we have learned about the human brain over the past two decades far surpasses the knowledge we had previously acquired. Our approaches to education need to catch up and stay caught up with our understanding of how the mind works.

Of course, as enticing and practically oriented as this idea sounds, we recognize that there is not a direct, easy path from knowing how the brain works to translating that knowledge into effective classroom practices or governance of educational systems. As Medina himself has noted, all brains are wired differently, so jumping from a brain rule to classroom rule can result in serious errors. Even so, we would be remiss if we did not greatly expand upon nascent efforts to understand how brain science might help us deliver better results for our students—and perhaps avoid serious harm. The urgency to do this is growing rapidly as we consider how some of the technologies we have noted—intelligent search, artificial intelligence, brain-computer interfaces—come to play a greater and greater role in education.

Cognitive scientist Daniel Willingham has suggested the possibility of an epidemiological approach to understanding the long-term impact of classroom practices and curricula on students.[51] Game-based learning expert Clark Aldrich has made a similar argument for "clinical trials" similar to those the pharmaceutical industry is required to conduct to prove the safety and effectiveness of its product.[52] We strongly advocate wide-scale implementation of such research with the connection between the brain, learning, and new technologies playing a key role.

Infrastructure and the Physical Plant

The school building of tomorrow must be extremely different from the ones that exist today. As articulated in the next chapter, we believe that a full integration of the physical school into the community will become an essential reality given many of the current and foreseeable dynamics of society today. This integration begins with abolishing the physical boxlike structure that characterizes most of our current schools. The direction in which we have pointed with each of the previous categories demands this change:

- Technology advances not only greatly reduce the need for physical infrastructure like traditional classrooms and libraries, they ensure that the majority of learning activity going forward will happen across digital networks and not within four walls.
- The need to move beyond traditional calendar structures and concepts such as standardized grade levels demands dramatically more fluidity in how groups of students and teachers are able to come together in meaningful ways.
- To finally embrace the reality of delivering a curriculum experience that truly serves student needs, smaller classes along with more group- and project-oriented work requires getting rid of the rows and rows of stationary desks within unmovable walls that are at the core of our current school infrastructure.
- The lessons we are learning about how the brain works, and the need to test and research thoroughly as we go forward, demand a diversity of experiences and physical environments that are tenable within the fixed nature of our current schools.

Everything about shedding the boxlike thinking that shapes our current approach to education demands a change in the physical structure and appearance of our institution, and in some cases—given what technology makes possible—the physical side of education will disappear entirely.

There are already numerous examples of how the physical side of education has been rethought to varying degrees, from innovative new designs for highly flexible, mobile desks by firms like Steelcase, to student-driven school designs by organizations like Big Picture Learning. We will look at other examples in the following chapter, but the bottom line is that as we build the communications, energy, and transportation grids for this century, innovative approaches to school design will play an integral role. We must sit at the planning table to insist that educational institutions be thought of first for a change. We cannot hope to break the mentality of the "box" if education continues to be thought of as planned for and considered separately from these other areas. We have shown that education has lagged behind the rest of society. Now, as we face the huge task of a complete upgrade and transformation of our infrastructural landscape, educators must sit at the planning table.

PREPARING TEACHERS

One inevitable outcome of the transformation process and the types of changes suggested here is that we must revamp how we educate and train our teachers. Successfully navigating and managing the range of issues highlighted in this chapter requires skills and knowledge that go well beyond those that sufficed in the traditional classroom environment. Efforts to increase teacher accountability—the focus of many educational reformers—will be of little value if we are not prepared to provide the educational and professional development experiences that address the educational demands of the twenty-first century.

We have said relatively little about teachers throughout this book primarily because we do not agree that they are the scapegoat, as they are often made to be, for our broader educational problems. Most teachers, in our experience, are as dedicated to the idea of providing high-quality education as the most zealous reformers. But we must be prepared to support them, both by transforming the context in which they do their work and by providing them with appropriate opportunities for building the new skills and knowledge this context demands. A vision of transformation of the entire K–12 education system necessitates a similar effort in the higher education and professional development programs where teachers are prepared for this new landscape.

YOUR CONTRIBUTION

In the next chapter, we offer an expanded vision for education in the twenty-first century, but even as we move forward with the vision, we must continue asking and wrestling with the questions—that is the nature of life and change in the Shift Age. To encourage collaboration and facilitate many voices contributing to this dialogue, we designed the website for the book— www.shiftedtransformation.com—to offer many opportunities for readers to post resources as well as ask and reply to questions. We encourage you to visit the site, offer other questions that must be asked, and help develop deeper answers to the quick ones we have written here.

We now turn toward the future and an expanded vision of twenty-first-century education.

KEY POINTS

- Shift Ed begins with asking fundamental questions that must be answered. We have grouped these questions into five categories:
  - Technology and connectivity
  - Calendar and operations

- o Curriculum
- o Learning and the brain
- o Infrastructure and the physical plant

- Some directions in which we might go in each of these areas include:
  - o Technology and connectivity: open up to a much higher level of connectivity in our schools and help our children acquire the skills necessary for using the technology effectively.
  - o Calendar and operations: abolish year-based grade levels and end the Agricultural Age practice of summer vacation.
  - o Curriculum: move the content versus skills debate rapidly forward and commit to supporting the types of learning environments and experiences that we already know to be effective.
  - o Learning and the brain: make a significant commitment to more research on connecting knowledge about the brain to effective learning practices.
  - o Infrastructure and the physical plant: end the tyranny of the box and broadly implement more flexible approaches to school design.

- Ask more questions and contribute to the answers at www .shiftedtransformation.com.

CHANGE VISIONS

Survival Skills for the Twenty-First Century

Tony Wagner is co-director of the Change Leadership Group at the Harvard Graduate School of Education. The themes discussed here are discussed more fully in his book The Global Achievement Gap: Why Even Our Best Schools Don't Teach the New Survival Skills Our Children Need—and What We Can Do About It.

Across the United States, I see schools that are succeeding at making adequate yearly progress but failing our students. Increasingly, there is only one curriculum: test prep. Of the hundreds of classes that I've observed in recent years, fewer than one in twenty was engaged in instruction designed to teach students to think instead of merely drilling for the test.

While schools are focused on drills, I have yet to talk to a recent graduate, college teacher, community leader, or business leader who said that not knowing enough academic content was a problem. So what are they saying we need? My research suggests there are seven survival skills our students need to thrive in today's world.

1. Critical Thinking and Problem Solving

To compete in the new global economy, companies need their workers to think about how to continuously improve their products, processes, or services. Over and over, executives told me that the heart of critical thinking and problem solving is the ability to ask the right questions. As one senior executive from Dell said, "Yesterday's answers won't solve today's problems."

2. Collaboration and Leadership

Teamwork is no longer just about working with others in your building. Christie Pedra, CEO of Siemens, explained, "Technology has allowed for virtual teams. We have teams working on major infrastructure projects that are all over the U.S. On other projects, you're working with people all around the world on solving a software problem. Every week they're on a variety of conference calls; they're doing webcasts; they're doing net meetings."

3. Agility and Adaptability

Clay Parker explained that anyone who works at BOC Edwards today "has to think, be flexible, change, and use a variety of tools to solve new problems. We change what we do all the time. I can guarantee the job I hire someone to do will change or may not exist in the future, so this is why adaptability and learning skills are more important than technical skills."

4. Initiative and Entrepreneurialism

Mark Chandler, senior vice president and general counsel at Cisco, was one of the strongest proponents of initiative: "I say to my employees, if you try five things and get all five of them right, you may be failing. If you try 10 things, and get eight of them right, you're a hero. You'll never be blamed for failing to reach a stretch goal, but you will be blamed for not trying. One of the problems of a large company is risk aversion. Our challenge is how to create an entrepreneurial culture in a larger organization."

5. Effective Oral and Written Communication

Mike Summers of Dell said, "We are routinely surprised at the difficulty some young people have in communicating: verbal skills, written skills, presentation skills. They have difficulty being clear and concise; it's hard for them to create focus, energy, and passion around the points they want to make." Summers and other leaders from various companies were not necessarily complaining about young people's poor grammar, punctuation, or spelling—the things we spend so much time teaching and testing in our schools. Although writing and speaking correctly are obviously important, the complaints I heard most frequently were about fuzzy thinking and young people not knowing how to write with a real voice.

6. Accessing and Analyzing Information

Employees in the twenty-first century have to manage an astronomical amount of information daily. It's not only the sheer quantity of information that represents a challenge, but also how rapidly the information is changing. Quick—how many planets are there? In the early 1990s, I heard then–Harvard University president Neil Rudenstine say in a speech that the half-life of knowledge in the humanities is ten years, and in math and science, it's only two or three years. I wonder what he would say it is today.

7. Curiosity and Imagination

Daniel Pink, the author of *A Whole New Mind,* observes that with increasing abundance, people want unique products and services: "For businesses it's no longer enough to create a product that's reasonably priced and adequately functional. It must also be beautiful, unique, and meaningful."[1] Pink notes that developing young people's capacities for imagination, creativity, and empathy will be increasingly important for maintaining the United States' competitive advantage in the future. Mike Summers at Dell told me, "People who've learned to ask great questions and have learned to be inquisitive are the ones who move the fastest in our environment because they solve the biggest problems in ways that have the most impact on innovation."

Meeting the Need

Teaching students in a way that arms them properly with the seven skills is not at all beyond our current knowledge or capabilities, but it doesn't happen with anything close to consistency in our existing education system. Once in a great while, I observe a class in which it does happen, and it looks something like this:

At the beginning of the period in an algebra class, the teacher writes a problem on the board. He turns to the students, who are sitting in desks arranged in squares of four that face one another. "You haven't seen this kind of problem before," he explains. "Solving it will require you to use concepts from both geometry and algebra. Each group will try to develop at least two different ways to solve this problem. After all the groups have finished, I'll randomly choose someone from each group who will write one of your proofs on the board, and I'll ask that person to explain the process your group used."

The groups quickly go to work. Animated discussion takes place as students pull the problem apart and talk about different ways to solve it. While they work, the teacher circulates from group to group. When a student asks a question, the teacher responds with another question:

---

[1]Pink, D. (2005, pp. 32–33)

"Have you considered . . . ?" "Why did you assume that?" or simply "Have you asked someone in your group?"

What makes this an effective lesson—a lesson in which students are learning a number of the seven survival skills while also mastering academic content? First, students are given a complex, multistep problem that is different from any they've seen in the past. To solve it, they have to apply critical-thinking and problem-solving skills and call on previously acquired knowledge from both geometry and algebra. Mere memorization won't get them far. Second, they have to find two ways to solve the problem, which requires initiative and imagination. Third, they have to explain their proofs using effective communication skills. Fourth, the teacher does not spoon-feed students the answers. He uses questions to push students' thinking and build their tolerance for ambiguity. Finally, because the teacher announces in advance that he'll randomly call on a student to show how the group solved the problem, each student in every group is held accountable. Success requires teamwork.

As this example suggests, we need to use academic content to teach the seven survival skills every day, at every grade level, and in every class. In addition, we need to insist on a combination of locally developed assessments and new nationally normed, online tests—such as the College and Work Readiness Assessment (www.cae.org)—that measure students' analytic-reasoning, critical-thinking, problem-solving, and writing skills.

But to teach and test the skills that our students need, we must first redefine excellent instruction. It is not a checklist of teacher behaviors and a model lesson that covers content standards. It is working with colleagues to ensure that all students master the skills they need to succeed as lifelong learners, workers, and citizens.

It's time to hold ourselves and all of our students to a new and higher standard of rigor, defined according to twenty-first-century criteria. It's time for our profession to advocate for accountability systems that will enable us to teach and test the skills that matter most. Our students' futures are at stake.

Expand the Vision

We should try to be the parents of our future, rather than the offspring of our past.

—Miguel de Unamuno

All significant paths of discovery, invention, and yes, transformation begin with the understanding of what is. Next, the questions as to what is needed or how things should be addressed are raised and used to expand the thinking of all in the endeavor. Once enough time is spent in attempting to answer the long list of critical questions, then we face forward and begin the task of birthing our future, parenting a new reality and leaning into the challenge and extreme effort needed to forge the new vision.

THE NEW VISION OF EDUCATION FOR THE TWENTY-FIRST CENTURY

We now offer a vision for education that builds on four fundamental concepts. This vision is not complete: the questions asked in the prior chapter will no doubt spark many more questions as well as a wide variety of potential answers. We hope you will add to this dialogue, whether at our website (www.shiftedtransformation.com) or in any of the other places where you find yourself thinking and talking about education. We have tried, however, to anticipate as many questions and answers as possible and roll them up into the four key areas that we see essential. If we can find the wisdom, general unanimity, resolve, and collective vision to mobilize a massive amount of human and financial commitment to these four areas, we should at least be on the right journey together.

FOUR FUNDAMENTALS FOR TWENTY-FIRST-CENTURY EDUCATION

We identify four fundamental concepts that will drive educational transformation in the coming decades:

1. The community-centric school

2. The five Cs

3. Shape shifting

4. A simple collective choice

Some of these relate to how education is designed and delivered, while some relate to our perspectives on education and change. While each concept is important on its own, moving forward with them in concert is the only way to achieve the ultimate goal of transformation.

The Community-Centric School

The schools of this new century must be *community centric.* The education of our young must take place in a much more integrated way with the communities they will be a part of as adults. There are two communities into which schools must be fully integrated: the physical, local community in which they serve children daily; and the virtual, global community to which they connect.

The Local Community

Children grow up and live their day-to-day lives in actual physical communities. They develop a sense of who they are as individuals largely in relation to these communities. If, as we have argued, individuals today have more power than individuals have ever had in history—the Flow to the Individual force of the Shift Age—then the role of the community is critical: to a significant degree the local community in which a child grows up and is educated shapes who this child becomes as an individual. The human, high-touch interactions a physical community offers in this increasingly high-tech world provides a foundation for life.

Earlier in this book we commented on how isolated and segregated our schools often are from their communities. We have all seen large suburban schools set apart from the populace and surrounded by fences. Is it a factory, a jail, or a high school? This separateness creates many more problems than it solves. It is time to put schools at the center of their local communities.

Currently a big high school or elementary school building sits largely idle for ten to twelve hours of the day, five days a week, and all day on the weekends. The classrooms are empty, the playing fields and athletic facilities are empty, the library is empty, and the security is on. At a minimum, much greater use of these facilities should be made to provide adult education experiences in the evenings and host a wide variety of community events that can bring children, their families, and other members of the community together in meaningful ways. Parents themselves may be among the learners who take advantage of the range of adult learning offerings that could be housed in schools—a model of lifelong learning that would serve as a great example for the children.

Carrying this line of thinking further, there is no reason that community libraries, community centers, and community colleges could not all share a common infrastructure. Currently, each of these institutions typically has its own budget, its own buildings, and its own bureaucracy. Even leaving aside the other benefits of deeper connection and integration, in an age of shrinking funding, for each of these institutions to exist in a silo is madness.

Going yet a step further, schools could play an integral role in helping to address the health care crisis that afflicts our nation. Currently, most schools have minimal health facilities. The only question that gets addressed is whether the child is too ill to stay in school that day. At a minimum, we should encourage the availability of primary health care providers in the schools for a few hours, but it would also make a great deal of sense for there to be health care facilities permanently colocated with school facilities. Both child and parent would benefit from greater ease of access, and greater integration of health care access and health care education could help us make tremendous strides to combat growing problems like childhood obesity and related diseases like diabetes.

Going the final step, we should move toward school facilities that are not separated at all from other parts of our communities, including the places where we shop and do business. Imagine a thriving hub at the center of a community that incorporates the previous elements with the ability to access other basic activities of everyday life like shopping for groceries, getting a haircut, renewing a drivers license, or picking up clothes at the dry cleaners. This is the sort of forward-thinking community design that brings school back into life. And if we lay aside the old model of the school as a mass-production factory system, there is no reason that education cannot fit fluidly into such a design.

Approaching the integration of education and community in this way addresses at least two significant issues.

First, it helps alleviate the detachment from community life that often leads to social alienation and some of its worst symptoms—like the rise of gangs in communities. Children would naturally see themselves—and be seen, literally—as part of the community, rather than as a part of the population to be "dealt with" by being shipped off to special facilities for six to ten hours out of the day. We would move much closer to realizing the wise old African saying that "it takes a village to raise a child." Just substitute *community* for village.

Second, an approach to education that unites currently disparate institutions and places them squarely in the midst of everyday community activity could have a dramatic impact on our ability to meet the educational demands of the coming decade. To meet the demand for education in the coming decades, we need to build large numbers of new schools. But how likely does that seem given the budget straits we currently face and seem to continually face when it comes to the question of sufficiently funding education? There is no reason, of course, that existing office spaces or libraries or parts of community centers could not be used for teaching our children. The main force preventing such a change is our current enthrallment with the factory school models of the past and the related idea that children must be shipped off to a large box each day for education to happen.

There are already good examples of schools moving in the direction described here. Glen Oak High School in Canton, Ohio, for example, features an integrated public library, an urgent care facility, and a range of other design elements to support learning and attract community interaction.[53] The group of innovative charter schools started by Big Picture Learning emphasize "learning in the real world," an approach to providing all students with internships and mentoring in real organizations during their school year.[54] The Coalition for Community Schools has made significant strides in supporting the growth of community-centered schools across the United States, schools that "become centers of the community and are open to everyone."[55] Each of these groups and many others work independently to create more community-focused schools. We need to give local school systems across the country the power and resources they need to think in similar, innovative ways about their schools, and encourage them to pursue community-centric models.

We realize, of course, that critics will say such approaches simply are not replicable on a large scale and cannot be implemented in our most problematic communities, but such criticism assumes that we must create a monolithic, standardized model to which every school conforms. There is absolutely nothing, other than our own preconceptions and prejudices, to support this view. Education thought leader Yong Zhao, in reply to those who emphasize standardization and scalability, draws a useful analogy between schools and restaurants. While we have tended to think of our schools using a "fast food" model—which seemingly offers the benefit of churning out schools and their end products, students, rapidly and with little variation—we might better think of them as Chinese restaurants. There are, as Zhao points out, no large Chinese restaurant chains and no centralized set of operational standards.[56] Each restaurant is free to serve customers in a way that matches its particular circumstances and unique abilities, and yet we know basically what to expect when we walk into a Chinese restaurant in any town in the United States. Community-integrated schools would thrive based on a similar philosophy.

The Global Community

Not only do schools need to connect more tightly with local communities, they need to connect to the world. Our children, now and for the rest of their lives, will live in a global community. We have entered the global stage of human evolution. The economy is global; electronic connectivity is global. There are no longer the limitations of time and place on human communication that existed when current education systems were developed. This is the new landscape of humanity. This is the manifestation of the Flow to Global of the Shift Age. The school of this century must be also centered in this global community.

A global-centric school must have global connectivity, a more globally oriented curriculum, and a process that provides children with a sense of self within this global landscape. This does not mean that relationship to one's state or country is to be downplayed or that state or national history and culture should be diminished. It means that in addition to such teaching there must also be a new emphasis on being a global citizen and being part of the emerging global culture.

Children today know this perhaps better than many adults. Many children have "friends" on Facebook from around the world. Inhabitants of the K–12 education system are the first children to grow up with awareness of global climate change. Multiple ethnicities are much more common today in schools than fifty years ago. We must build on this reality with connectivity and informed education. Indeed, in many ways, because it has been such a magnet for immigrants from other countries, the United States is uniquely positioned to learn from and leverage the diversity represented by the new global community. Our children are more and more often exposed to other cultures and other languages not only online but right in their communities. Whatever challenges the integration of other languages and cultures may bring, we must also realize that it brings tremendous opportunities.

We must realize and teach our children to understand that they live in two communities, the local community in which they live most of the time and the global community of humanity that will touch and affect them for the rest of their lives. Practically speaking, this means fully realizing the opportunities that cultural diversity in our local communities represent, but it also means actively using technology to connect students and classrooms across the globe for project-based work and sharing of stories and perspective related to the key issues and opportunities of our day. It is potentially a time of great opportunity for organizations like Sister Cities International that can help different communities of the world connect both online and off.

There is little doubt that the vision of a global electronic village has become a reality, and it is becoming even more so every day. The school is the childhood institution that must play a key role in preparing children for this new global community.

Connection

 While more fully bringing schools into the life of our communities will no doubt present many challenges, it is one of the most powerful catalysts for transforming K–12 education. Aside from making it possible to better leverage and share community resources, this approach also lends natural support to the next fundamental of Shift Ed: the five Cs.

The Five Cs

For two hundred years, the shorthand for K–12 education was the three Rs—reading, (w)riting, and (a)rithmetic. We now must add the *five Cs*:

1. Creativity

2. Collaboration

3. Critical thinking

4. Content

5. Context

It is these five ideas that must become core components in twenty-first-century education.

Creativity

Forward-thinking educators now see how the legacy, manufacturing model of K–12 education can drain creativity from our children as they move through the grade-by-grade assembly line. Visionaries and educators such as Sir Ken Robinson have pointed out that children start out naturally creative (when was the last time you played make believe?)

but that we systematically siphon creativity away as we process them to become "brains" or "academic overachievers."[57] This may not have been a problem in the Industrial Age, when the current education system evolved, as creativity was not highly valued for a life in the factory or the office or in economies that operated on both productivity and scarcity. But in the Shift Age, where change is environmental, innovation is a primary economic driver, and information is of less value than the ways it can be used, creativity is essential.

To be successful in the twenty-first century, each of us must be able to see the problems of the world clearly and find creative solutions, to assimilate avalanches of information and find creative ways to selectively use and combine information to create new realities, situations, products, and solutions. Not surprisingly, a recent IBM survey of 1,500 CEOs identified creativity as the "single most important leadership competency" for the complex times in which we currently live—and which will only become more complex in the future.[58] Creativity will be a quality that increases in importance every day from now on.

A primary goal of twenty-first-century education must be the development of human creativity. We have known for some time now how to do this—for example, through smaller classroom environments where more students can actively participate or through project-based work focused on discovery and problem solving—but we have so far lacked the collective will to make it happen. The community-integrated approach to schooling that we advocate would, we believe, do much more to support active learning in smaller groups than our mass-production school systems do, and advances in technology can also play a vital role. Take, for example, the way in which increasing numbers of students use a tool like Scratch, developed by the Lifelong Kindergarten Group at the MIT Media Lab (http://scratch.mit.edu). Scratch is a simple programming language that enables young children to create interactive stories, animations, games, music, and art, and then share them on the web. At the time we are writing this book, there are already more than a million projects created by more than 150,000 young people around the world. The possibilities for children using a tool like this—a tool that would have been beyond the reach, if not beyond the imagination of teachers just a generation ago—are phenomenal. And in addition to providing a powerful creative outlet that supports multiple learning skills, Scratch is also a shining example of the power of the next of the five Cs on our list: collaboration.

Collaboration

Twenty years ago, it would have been inconceivable to most people that a venerable institution like the Encyclopedia Britannica could be overthrown by an unpaid group of individuals devoted to providing open access to knowledge online. Nor would most people have believed that the seeds of the record industry's downfall would be sown by a college student with a relatively simple program for allowing individual computer users to easily share their music files with others. And newspaper, magazine, and book publishing executives certainly didn't foresee the rise of the web as a massive self-publishing engine that would undermine the existence of print media.

But all of these things happened. Jimmy Wales and his band of "rag tag" followers—as he puts it—built Wikipedia. Shawn Fanning, as a student at Northeastern University, launched Napster. And Web 2.0 came along and provided pretty much everyone with the ability to say—and report on—pretty much whatever they wanted whenever they wanted to. Collaboration, whether more or less formal, but on a massive scale, made it all possible. This same sort of collaboration is possible for schoolchildren using a wide range of free or low-cost tools—including the Scratch application.

Humanity now collaborates at unprecedented levels. Connectivity has allowed us to collaborate without any limitations of time and place. In addition to the ability to create entirely new business models—and destroy old ones—we can work with anyone, anywhere, at any time and on practically anything. Perhaps most important for education, collaboration—through approaches like crowd sourcing and technology-supported social learning—is now a way to knowledge. Indeed, some have begun to argue convincingly that knowledge *is* the network.[59] All of these changes are relatively recent, but they are clearly here to stay and must therefore be brought more fully into the process of education as soon as possible.

Collaboration is an essential part of the world in this new century. Many fields of endeavor have become so complex that only through the collaboration of individuals can new solutions and products be created. Humanity is facing global problems—like climate change and regulation of global markets—that can only collaborative interaction can solve. In a recent survey of 342 organizations, 75 percent indicated that they have put collaboration tools in place to support work by employees.[60] In developed countries, nearly every child who graduates from high school in the coming decade will be required to engage in collaborative activities—many of them online—to earn a living.

We have occasionally trained our children to work together on a project, to study together in a group, to share in scientific experiments. All of that is well and good and should continue—but we must take it further and make it central to how we teach. We must now consciously cultivate the art, science, practice, and experience of collaboration in every area of education, not just occasionally in the classroom or on the courts and playing fields. Students who can combine creativity with collaborative effort will be the problem solvers and leaders of tomorrow. In fact, it could be said that the major problems of humanity on spaceship earth will not be solved without a high level of creative collaboration. Education must endeavor to serve this reality.

Critical Thinking

Anyone who has been a parent or spent much time around very young children knows that they are capable of asking "why?" incessantly. As annoying as the question can become, it is an incredibly useful and important one for making sense of the world. Unfortunately, as we grow older, it is a question that most of us ask less and less. As children, we enter our educational system virtually bursting with curiosity, and twelve years later too many of us exit it pretty well resigned to things as they are.

The draining of inquisitiveness from our students may seem merely regrettable, but in the world in which we now live, it is much more than that: it is dangerous. Each of us as individuals now receives more information from more sources and with greater speed and frequency than has ever been the case before in human history. Vast quantities of that information are irrelevant, biased, or flat-out wrong. Some of it is even harmful. If we do not teach our children how to ask the right questions and effectively analyze and make judgments about the information they receive, we leave them open to a wide range of deception and abuse.

Rote learning—simply committing a body of content and concepts to memory—used to be the way to knowledge. It now is only a small part of that path. When a few keystrokes on a handheld device can provide access to most of human knowledge, the relentless memorization of fragments of this knowledge increasingly becomes a waste of time. If known information and knowledge is seconds away, then what one is capable of doing with that information and knowledge becomes the issue. To bolster critical thinking, learning in our schools needs to be driven much more by projects and group work that require children to ask questions and solve problems; that encourage them to analyze information, recognize patterns, and draw meaningful conclusions; and that guide them toward engaging with real-life situations. The current regimen of drills, standardized homework, and preparation for tests often does exactly the opposite.

Content

In current and past educational systems, content has meant facts, information, and methods. Again, the three Rs have been the foundation. Each level of education layered more content upon the prior level, filling up the vessel of the mind. We must now broaden the educational definition of content and reconsider the role of both student and teacher in relation to content.

The Information Age spawned the cliché that "content is king." Those who created, owned, controlled, and licensed content had power. Those who effectively used the content they had learned were rewarded. In this paradigm, teachers are often perceived as little more than intermediaries, and as a result, hold relatively little power or influence outside of the limited sphere of formal education. While content will always play a critical role in education—it is, after all, difficult to learn without learning about *something*—our educational approaches must recognize that the old dynamics of content are quickly losing their relevance.

Content is no longer the static and highly protected object that it once was. The possibilities for accessing, reusing, remixing, and altering content are now infinite. And perhaps of even greater importance, the tools for content production and distribution are now firmly in the hands of the masses rather than the privileged—and well-capitalized—few. It would be difficult to overestimate the impact this change will have over the long term. The possibilities for creating, accessing, reusing, altering, remixing, and otherwise manipulating content of nearly every type are now infinite. Napster and Wikipedia, both already referenced, are early examples. The rise in popularity of "mash-ups," which pull together images, video, and audio from multiple sources, are another.

Increasingly, students must know how to participate in this new environment of content effectively, both by being producers and—as already suggested—by having the skills to consume with an appropriate level of judgment. At the same time, teachers need an entirely new skill set for effectively managing content as part of their work. They, too, must learn to be producers, and more important, they must learn to be effective "curators" of content for their students: they must have the skills necessary for sourcing the best types of content to support their teaching and facilitate meaningful access to this content in much the same way that a highly skilled museum creator transforms artifacts into an engaging learning experience for visitors.

The web is packed with a vast array of content accessible by teachers and students alike, but a particularly important resource is the vast library of open educational content published by institutions and individual contributors around the world over the past several years. Ranging from videos, to articles, to interactive exercises, to syllabi—just to name a few possibilities—open education resources (OER) represent a huge reservoir of educational content that can be accessed freely and used, in most cases, under the broad terms of licensing models like those pioneered by Creative Commons (http://www.creativecommons.org). At the time this book is being written, the OER Commons, one of the leading sites dedicated to aggregating open educational resources, lists more than 20,000 resources available for primary and secondary education. Similarly, Kahn Academy (http://www .khanacademy.org/) provides more than 1,800 (and growing rapidly) freely accessible videos that cover a wide range of topics typically included in K–12 curricula. In a world where funding is tight but education increasingly needs to be customized to smaller groups of students, this is a huge boon. But truly taking advantage of it requires abilities for finding, assessing, and managing content unlike what has ever been necessary before.

In this sort of dynamic environment, it no longer seems appropriate to think of content as "king"—the throne has been usurped by a new ruler: context.

Context

In this new century, in this new age, a new phrase is becoming true: "context is king."

The world is rapidly changing and change is environmental— it is everywhere, all around us, every day. Unlike past ages when the context of agriculture or manufacturing was relatively fixed, the context of the Shift Age is a state of variable rates of shift. We must integrate an understanding of context into our education system, beginning with how our students engage with learning content, but extending ultimately into how they engage with life. To not do so will only amplify the disconnect between the context of the outdated classroom and the dynamically changing society outside the classroom.

With an overwhelming amount of information and content washing over us on a daily basis, it is now the ability to establish context and command attention that creates value. In the classroom—as in nearly every other part of life—this means much less of a "push" approach in which the content to be mastered is thrust upon the student and much more of a "pull" approach that establishes relevance and taps into each individual learner's motivation. Integrating our schools more closely into the communities they serve would be a major step toward creating a more meaningful context for learning, but it is a shift that must be supported by teachers who are skilled in creating and facilitating the best possible contexts for learning—ones that do not rely upon the worn-out, stand-and-deliver approach that has alienated countless students over the years.

Ultimately, teachers must help students become *masters of context*—people who are able to curate content, engage with it critically, creatively, and collaboratively, and offer up insights and solutions. Those who will hold the best jobs, at the highest pay in the coming decades, must have this capability. Those who will lead our organizations and communities and help solve the myriad problems we now face also must have these capability. In truth, it is a capability that will be required of anyone who wishes to live a productive and fulfilling life in this new age.

There is one important twist though: to be a master of context is not a one-time event—it is a capability that individuals, organizations, and even entire societies need to invoke again and again as they change shape to meet the demands of a rapidly evolving world.

Connection

Clearly each of the five Cs would be strongly supported by having community-centric schools. Creativity is enhanced by access to a greater variety of resources and modes of expression. Collaboration will clearly be enhanced as students interact with a wider range of individuals as well as nonclassroom aspects of both the local and global communities. Critical thinking will be bolstered as students have the opportunity to work with adults in the community on solving everyday problems and wrestling with possible solutions to larger issues. Content, in the community-centric model, is not simply the content of textbooks and lectures, but rather the real-life content of the community in which children live along with the vast amount of content—including self-produced and collaboratively produced content—available as part of the global community. Finally, the community *is* context in a much more relevant way than a classroom can ever be. In a community-centered approach to schooling, the growing importance of assessing and understanding knowledge in context is no longer an abstract exercise—it becomes a vital part of the student's twenty-first-century life.

The creation of the community-centric school and the clear transformation of the curricula that will occur when the five Cs are fully embraced will lead right into the third fundamental of Shift Ed: shape shifting.

Shape Shifting

The ability to change form—to *shape shift*—has served as a "solution" to seemingly unsolvable problems in countless mythical plots throughout the ages. One of the most recent examples—and one familiar to so many children worldwide—can be found in the highly popular Harry Potter books, but countless writers, ancient shamans, and not so ancient gurus have spoken of the ability to rapidly change from one type of being into another. It is a concept woven deeply into humanity, and as mystical and otherworldly as it may sound, it is one that needs to be woven equally deeply into our concept of education—and life—as we move forward.

If the world is indeed changing as rapidly as we claim—and there is plenty of evidence in addition to what is presented here to suggest that it is—then individuals, institutions, and even entire societies must be prepared to adapt rapidly new demands. Because technology and other systemic forces that can be controlled only in limited ways increasingly drive change, we cannot assume that we will be able to slow down or alter our direction if the change proves not to be to our liking. Huge numbers of people have already found that in our current economy their roles have become obsolete or replaceable by cheaper labor or technologies. There is no going back to what they had. The only way these people can survive—much less thrive—is if they can shape shift into new roles by acquiring new capabilities. There is every reason to expect the need to rapidly adjust in this way will grow dramatically in the future.

Our children, therefore, must learn the capability of shape shifting if they are to enjoy any level of stability in their lives. Fortunately, the type of shape shifting we advocate does not require a wand or other magical implements. Indeed, two of the major tools are already widely available:

- Access to knowledge at high speed—through increasingly powerful search and knowledge management strategies, by connecting to others through social knowledge networks
- Access to resources quickly—though outsourcing, collaboration, and potentially robotics and artificial intelligence

We now need to apply the concepts articulated earlier in this chapter to enable children to use these tools effectively to acquire new capabilities and transform themselves as new challenges and opportunities arise.

Part of the reason for teaching our children these skills is so that they may apply them in their individual lives, but an equally important goal is for them to be able to apply them collaboratively in the organizations and societies where they work, live, and lead. We must be able to shift shape not only as individuals but also collectively as we move forward in an age of continuous and rapid change. We have already seen so many institutions from past centuries crumble as they have failed to shape their business model or processes to the times. Everything we create together going forward must have the qualities of shape shifting baked into them. Our physical schools must be created with adaptive designs, ones that can flow with the adaptations that the community will need to make over time. Our curricula must be based upon an ongoing need to morph. The vision of adulthood that we help our children develop must include a clear understanding of shifting to keep pace with the shifting shape of society. Across the board, as we create twenty-first-century education, we must constantly ask ourselves: how do we instill in our children, the future adults of our society, a fundamental ability to rapidly and radically adapt—to shape shift—as the need arises?

Connection

 It should be clear that this third fundamental of Shift Ed, shift shaping education, is a natural outcome of combining the community-centric school with the five Cs. All three of these Shift Ed fundamentals, though, cannot occur without the fourth fundamental: a simple collective choice. It is this fundamental that must be embraced immediately if we are to lead rather than be overwhelmed by the transformative opportunity of Shift Ed.

A Simple Collective Choice

While we often mention technology as a powerful force throughout this book, much of what we propose with respect to *leading* the transformation of education has little to do with technology. Nor, for the most part, do we suggest educational approaches aside from those already known to be effective. Technology has acquired a momentum of its own at this point, and will continue to evolve rapidly and change the world regardless of anything we do. And we already know a tremendous amount about what will make the education of our children more effective. We do not need to keep chasing fads and quick-fix reforms. No, what we need at this point is leadership, vision, and the triumph of our collective will.

There is nothing that says we cannot have schools that do not look like boxes. Nothing that says we cannot abolish traditional curricula and the nine-month school year. Nothing that says schools cannot exist less as physical structures and more as a continuous activity woven seamlessly into our communities. There is nothing that says this other than our own minds, minds that are enthralled with the past and fixated on perpetuating models that no longer serve our needs.

Part of the problem we currently face is that many important stakeholders still do not fully appreciate the challenge and its magnitude. For example, earlier in this book, we noted a Gallup poll showing that more than half of the American public feels the public education system is not doing its job. And yet, in that same poll, 76 percent of parents indicated they were satisfied with the education their own children receive in school. Gallup has been conducting this same poll since 1999, and the results have not varied widely over that time period. In general, people tend to be mostly satisfied with the education their own children are receiving but dissatisfied with the quality of education overall.

Addressing this sort of disconnect is critical if we hope to transform education in this country. As John Kotter, one of the world's most widely recognized authorities on change management, has asserted, significant change rarely occurs where there is not a sense of urgency,[61] and we are significantly less likely to feel urgency about matters that do not seem to impact us personally.

For most parents, the schooling their children are receiving looks very much like the schooling the parents themselves received. They grew up with a school year based on the agricultural calendar, with buildings and curricula designed for the Industrial Age. If all of this worked reasonably well in the past, why shouldn't it work now? Additionally, parents are closer to and naturally feel more in control of their own child's education than an abstract notion like "the state of schools." If there are problems, adjustments can be made. So long as homework gets done and grades are reasonably good, there's relatively little reason to worry.

But as we have shown repeatedly throughout this book, there is *plenty* of reason to worry. Our hope is that this book is part of an overall wake-up call to end the sort of unconscious complacency that infects not only parents but also other key stakeholders, including many teachers, administrators, and government officials. Most important, we hope it is a wake-up call that takes hold and spreads throughout the general public. Only when each of us wakes up and begins to feel the deep urgency of our current situation will the entrenched interests that favor the status quo begin to feel real pressure for change. Only then will we feel the urgency needed to achieve not just reform but true transformation.

We would not have written this book if we did not believe that transformation was possible. Indeed, as we argued earlier, we believe it is inevitable. The question is whether we choose to actively embrace and shape the transformation or simply allow ourselves to be shaped by it. We view this as a *simple collective choice.*

We commented earlier in this book on levels of the social spending of tax monies in various areas. As a society, we have embraced state-of-the-art weaponry that has the capacity to kill all humanity ten times over but we provide our children with a completely inadequate education. This has been our social choice, whether active or passive. It is within our collective power to choose differently.

We complain about taxes. We complain about our education system. We complain about career politicians primarily concerned with reelection. The history of our society provides plenty of examples to justify our complaints, but the future doesn't care. In order to create education systems for the twenty-first century we need the social commitment and the social funding to do so. This is a simple reality. Those of us who believe that educational transformation is essential must lead the way to bring about a simple, clear, collective choice to do so.

We recognize, of course, that there are many who will view this perspective as politically naïve, who will feel that the only way forward is by incremental change that assuages the myriad special interests involved in our education systems. We are not blind to the challenges inherent in the type of change we advocate, but we believe the time for incremental change has passed. As a society, as a country, as a species, the time has come to ask whether *we sincerely want to transform education*. We must answer that question with a loud collective "yes!" and then move forward rapidly together if we want to succeed.

KEY POINTS

There are four fundamentals to the expanded vision of Shift Ed:

- The community-centric school: schools must be more fully integrated into both local and global communities.
- The five Cs: an understanding and mastery of creativity, collaboration, critical thinking, content, and context are, more so than ever, critical to our children's future success.
- Shape shifting: people, institutions, and even entire societies must develop the skill of adapting rapidly and radically to the new circumstances in which they find themselves.
- A simple collective choice: we have the technology and the knowledge we need to lead a major transformation. The question is not whether we can do it, but whether we *will* do it. It is up to us—now!

Start Now!

I skate to where the puck is going to be.

—Wayne Gretsky

We now face forward to redefine and recreate education for the twenty-first century. *We* is the truly active pronoun in this process. As authors we hope we have persuaded you that nothing less than a new beginning will succeed. We also hope we have made it clear that we already have what we need to make that new beginning. We now call on all of you to mobilize, bang the drum loudly, and create a much larger collective "we" that can truly embark on this difficult, exciting, critically important, and transformative effort to face the future and build an entirely new educational model—a model that will serve the future of us all.

As daunting as the task may seem, it will hardly be the first time that we have worked collectively to transform our educational system. Even the approaches we have questioned in this book—most important the development of common schools in support of universal education—represented huge leaps forward in their time. We would not even be having the current conversation about education if not for the progress that these changes enabled. But a new age requires new approaches.

In recent history, the time of transformation that comes closest to what we now experience is the decade after the Soviet Union launched Sputnik in October 1957. Overly confident of its position as the world leader in science, the United States was shocked to find that it had fallen so far behind the Russians. The situation was not unlike the one in which we now find ourselves—the global landscape had shifted dramatically and it was no longer clear that we could maintain the leadership position we had come to enjoy. It has been universally acknowledged that the Sputnik launch triggered the space race and jump-started a decades-long emphasis on the teaching of math and science at all levels of education in the United States. In the context of the cold war, this country felt threatened, vulnerable, and challenged. Today, while there is no one symbol as clear and dramatic as a Sputnik—so far— we have similar feeling as we look at the new global economic landscape. We feel threatened as we see our educational rankings sink in comparison to other countries. The major reaction so far has been to put greater and greater emphasis on teaching and assessing math and science skills. This was an appropriate response to the Sputnik challenge, just as the implementation of common schools was an appropriate approach to building a new democracy in an industrial age. But it is an insufficient response to our current challenges. As we have argued, we do not need incremental, reactionary changes: we need transformation.

As a country we must rise to this occasion. National, state, and local political leaders must find a way to join in a collective vision of educational transformation—perhaps using this book as one tool for creating that collective vision. As citizens we must demand nothing less from our leaders, and if they won't lead transformation, we must vote in politicians who will. Additionally, we must all take steps as individual citizens, parents, taxpayers, and educators to start making changes on a daily basis—now.

How can we do this when it seems that the problems with our educational system are so massive it is hard to even find a way to begin?

There are useful lessons to be learned from how our thinking about the environment has evolved over the past several years, and in particular to the work that Al Gore did to spread his message of "an inconvenient truth." Global warming, the issue at the heart of Gore's famous slide show presentation, is clearly a highly complex phenomenon, and not an easy issue to address. But it was also an issue that demanded attention if we were to avoid the serious consequences of inaction. Gore's presentation was a call to action on a global level to make immediate and fundamental changes to save our planet from overheating and substantial climate change. The key to its power was the central idea that dealing with climate change was an "inconvenience"—in other words, we know what to do, we just can't be bothered to do it.

Framing the issue in this way (along with a great deal of admirable persistence on Gore's part) dramatically increased the pressure on government and business to get serious about combating global warming through policy changes and a focus on environmentally friendly operations. Just as important—indeed, perhaps more so—it also inspired individual citizens to learn much more about climate change and—critically—to understand that they, too, could have an impact on the situation.

While pressing their governments to act, individuals could take actions daily, such as cutting use of electricity, buying more fuel-efficient cars, recycling more, changing their carbon footprints, and buying products that were more green than others. Everyone could do something that addressed the larger issue of "an inconvenient truth" and therefore feel empowered as part of the solution. Small steps could be taken daily while waiting for the larger policy issues to be put in place.

What we currently face in education is a similar inconvenient truth. There is no denying that the education of the youth of an entire country is a complex issue. But there is also no denying that something is broken, and simultaneously, powerful new dynamics are changing the entire educational environment—with or without our consent. We don't have all of the answers, and we can't see everything the future will bring, but we know more than enough to step up and lead the process rather than simply be overwhelmed by the consequences of our inaction.

One of the things that we have found lacking, as we've undertaken our own journey to better understand the state of education in America, is a resource that makes it easy to understand and act on the key issues relevant to the current state of K–12 education. There are many good data sources, educators and policy makers with much deeper experience than we have written many fine books, and on a number of good websites, forward-thinking educators communicate and collaborate with each other around many of the issues raised here. But for the average citizen, business leader, parent, or politician, trying to understand the issues so that it is possible to act can be a daunting task.

We view this book as one small contribution to collective understanding—and we have kept it purposely as short as we felt it could be so that it can be read and reread relatively quickly. But we also know that this is a dynamic topic, one that will evolve even before this book is published. So, to help support the ongoing work of educational transformation, we developed the Shift Ed 21, a set of twenty-one resources "posts" that provide learning opportunities and action tools related to the major topics covered in this book.

THE SHIFT ED 21

The following is a high-level outline of the twenty-one items we cover in more detail on our website at www.shiftedtrans formation.com. On the page for each item, there are brief, high-value resources along with some questions to prompt discussion, reflection, and further exploration. A link for each follows in this section, and we encourage you to visit the link, comment, share the resources, and also create additional resources of your own. We view this as part of a collective effort to empower ourselves, bring about change, and elevate the effort of educational transformation as frustrations with the expected slow speed of change from our political, governmental, and educational institutions rise. A large part of our efforts, no doubt, requires persuading people who question our actions, ridicule them, or resist the changes we seek. Move forward armed with the quote from Schopenhauer with which we began this book:

In the revelation of any truth, there are three stages. In the first it is ridiculed. In the second it is resisted and in the third it is considered self-evident.

1. Gather Your Tools
    Transformation is an active process. In this post we suggest how to use some simple technology tools to engage in learning and dialogue with others.
    http://bit.ly/shifted21-1

2. Where We Are
    Resources to help rapidly understand—and share with others—how much the world has changed in the past decade.
    http://bit.ly/shifted21-2

3. Where We May Be Going
    A look at where humanity might be headed, given the accelerating speed of change in technology and other areas.
    http://bit.ly/shifted21-3

4. Education Across the Globe
    A quick view into how the United States compares to other countries in its approach to education.
    http://bit.ly/shifted21-4

5. The Future of Education
    A brief exploration of some key themes related to education in the twenty-first century.
    http://bit.ly/shifted21-5

6. Generations
Insights into different generations and how they can work together.
http://bit.ly/shifted21-6

7. Connecting the Classroom
Examples of K–12 classrooms where technology is used as an integral part of the learning experience.
http://bit.ly/shifted21-7

8. What We Know Works
Information on approaches to more effective learning that we already know work, but that we do not take advantage of consistently across our schools.
http://bit.ly/shifted21-8

9. Rethinking the Calendar
Perspectives on issues including the year-round school year, grade levels, and summer vacation.
http://bit.ly/shifted21-9

10. The Brain and Learning
Updates on recent research and practical application of brain science as it applies to learning.
http://bit.ly/shifted21-10

11. Outside the Box
Some examples of what schools that break the traditional factory-box approach look like.
http://bit.ly/shifted21-11

12. Integrating With the Community
Exploration of examples of schools that are integrating more tightly with the community than traditional schools.
http://bit.ly/shifted21-12

13. Cultivating Creativity
What if schools were charged with cultivating creativity? Thoughts and examples of how that might look.
http://bit.ly/shifted21-13

14. Inspiring Collaboration

A look at ways in which collaboration among students can make the classroom a more exciting and effective place.

http://bit.ly/shifted21-14

15. Games to Change the World

More about the valuable lessons children can learn—and possibly teach—from games.

http://bit.ly/shifted21-15

16. Thinking Critically

Resource to help gain a better understanding of critical thinking skills—and how to make them a bigger part of our children's education.

http://bit.ly/shifted21-16

17. Open Education

A brief overview of the amazing world of open educational resources.

http://bit.ly/shifted21-17

18. Shape Shifters in Action

Forget Harry Potter: examples of real-life shape shifting by individuals and organizations.

http://bit.ly/shifted21-18

19. Finding Your Voice

Tips on where and how to declare support for educational transformation.

http://bit.ly/shifted21-19

20. Making Change

Change doesn't come without focused effort and effective tools: resources to help make it happen at the local, state, and national levels.

http://bit.ly/shifted21-20

21. Continuing to Learn

Finishing the Shift Ed 21 doesn't mean you are finished learning: some tools and approaches to help you and your children become effective lifelong learners.

http://bit.ly/shifted21-21

Parting—But Not Final—Words

This new effort of Shift Ed, the transformation of K–12 and all aspects of education from cradle to grave, is every bit as big and every bit as important as all the great challenges from our history. We hope we have managed to contribute meaningfully to a new vision of education. We hope we have added to and expanded the collective vision of the community of people who will accept nothing less than transformative educational change. We know that we have set forth a contribution, but not the full answer. We commit ourselves and ask that you commit to embracing what we have presented, and ask that you build upon it to create the future we all want.

As part of the journey toward transformation, we encourage you, once again, to join us at the website that we have created to support this book as well as the entire concept of Shift Ed: www.shiftedtransformation.com. We hope that this site becomes just one of the many nodes for educational transformation.

We must succeed in this endeavor.

Shift Ed begins now!

Notes

Chapter 1

1. "New problem for unions" (1959)
2. cf. Herbst (1996)

Chapter 2

3. Toffler & Toffler (2006)
4. Toffler & Toffler (2006)
5. Gallup (2009)
6. Strong agreement is judged by a respondent selecting 7, 8, or 9 on a 9-point scale from "Not good at all" to "Absolutely the best."
7. Gates Foundation (2010)
8. Alliance for Excellent Education (2010)
9. Alliance for Excellent Education (2010)
10. Partnership for 21st Century Skills (2008, p. 8)
11. Wagner (2008)
12. Banchero (2010)
13. Bergstedt (n.d.)
14. Alliance for Excellent Education (2010)
15. ACT (2010, p. 9)
16. U.S. Department of Education, National Center for Education Statistics (2007)
17. Carnevale, Smith, & Strohl (2010, p. 1).
18. Johnson & Rochkind (2009, p. 4).
19. Aldrich (2010)
20. Carnevale, Smith, & Strohl (2010, p. 1).
21. Conference Board, Corporate Voices for Working Families, Partnership for 21st Century Skills, & Society for Human Resource Management (2006, p. 13).

22. Conference Board (2009, p. 1)

23. U.S. Department of Labor, Bureau of Labor Statistics (BLS) (2008). Note that the BLS does not actually track career changes owing to the difficulty in defining a "career."

24. U.S. Department of Education, Institute of Education Sciences, National Center for Education Statistics (2009b)

25. U.S. Department of Education, National Center for Education Statistics (2009b)

26. U.S. Department of Education, National Center for Education Statistics (2009b)

27. College Board (2010, p. 6)

28. Carnevale, Smith, & Strohl (2010, p. 4)

Chapter 3

29. Drucker (1993)

30. See Houle (2008) for a more detailed discussion.

Chapter 4

31. RAND (2003, p. 1)

32. Devaney (2009)

33. Howe (2010)

34. Gallup (2009)

35. Howe (2010)

36. Pew Research Center (2009)

37. Pew Research Center (2010)

38. Hais & Winograd (2008)

39. Greenberg (2008, p. 6)

40. Prensky (2010)

Chapter 5

41. Carnevale, Smith, & Strohl (2010, p. 4)

Chapter 6

42. See http://www.kipp.org/

43. See http://www.teachforamerica.org/

44. See http://www.classroomofthefuture.org/innovationawards.asp

Chapter 7

45. Manzo (2009)

46. See, for example, Hargittai, Fullerton, Menchen-Trevino, & Thomas (2010)

47. Holland (2009)

48. Von Drehle (2010)

49. "Some schools grouping" (2010)

50. Medina (2008, p. 2)

51. Willingham (2010)

52. Aldrich (2010)

Chapter 8

53. See http://www.plainlocal.org/school_home.aspx?school id=17

54. See   http://www.bigpicture.org/2008/11/learning-in-the-real-world-lti/

55. See http://www.communityschools.org/aboutschools/what_is_a_community_school.aspx

56. "Alan November interview" (2007)

57. Sir Ken Robinson (2007)

58. IBM (2010, p. 3)

59. See, for example, Siemens (2004)

60. Currier (2010)

61. Kotter (1996, pp. 35–49)

References

ACT (2010). *The condition of college & career readiness 2010.* Retrieved from http://www.act.org/research/policymakers/cccr10/pdf/ ConditionofCollegeandCareerReadiness2010.pdf.

Alan November interview, Dr. Yong Zhao, Part I. (2007, March. 10). *November Learning Podcast.* Podcast retrieved from http://itunes.apple .com/us/podcast/november-learning-podcast/id75128789.

Aldrich, C. (2010, July 24). Government agencies might want to do comprehensive clinical trials in education before it gives advice and creates standards. [Web log comment]. Retrieved from http://unschoolingrules.blogspot.com/2010/07/ask-govern ment-to-do-comprehensive.html.

Aldrich, C. (2010, June 19). If truth in advertising was applied to the school motto. [Web log comment]. Retrieved from http:// unschoolingrules.blogspot.com/2010/06/if-truth-in-advertising-was-applied-to.html.

Alliance for Excellent Education. (2010). *About the crisis.* Retrieved from http://www.all4ed.org/about_the_crisis.

Banchero, S. (2010, August 18). Scores stagnate at high schools. *Wall Street Journal.* Retrieved from http://online.wsj.com/article/ SB10001424052748703824304575435831555726858.html.

Baumert, K. A., Herzog, T., & Pershing, J. (2005) *Navigating the numbers: Greenhouse gas data and international climate policy.* Washington, DC: World Resources Institute. Retrieved February 22, 2011 from http://pdf.wri.org/navigating_numbers.pdf.

Bergstedt, J. (n.d.). *Thomas Jefferson's bill for universal education at the public expense.* Retrieved from http://jschell.myweb.uga.edu/ history/legis/jeffersonuniversal.htm.

Big Picture Learning. (n.d.). *Learning in the real world.* Retrieved from http://www.bigpicture.org/2008/11/learning-in-the-real-world-lti/.

Carnevale, A. P., Smith, N., & Strohl, J. (2010). *Help wanted: Projections of jobs and education requirements through 2018. Executive*

Summary. Washington, DC: Georgetown University Center on Education and the Workforce.

Coalition for Community Schools. (n.d.). *What is a community school?* Retrieved from http://www.communityschools.org/aboutschools/what_is_a_community_school.aspx.

College Board. (2010). *The College Completion Agenda 2010 progress report: Executive summary.* Retrieved from http://completion agenda .collegeboard.org/sites/default/files/reports_pdf/Progress_Exec utive_Summary.pdf.

Conference Board (2009). *The ill-prepared U.S. workforce: Exploring the challenges of employer-provided workforce readiness training. Key findings.* New York: Author.

Conference Board, Corporate Voices for Working Families, The Partnership for 21st Century Skills, and the Society for Human Resource Management. (2006). *Are they really ready to work? Employers' perspectives on the basic knowledge and applied skills of new entrants to the 21st century U.S. workforce.* New York: Author.

Currier, G. (2010, June 28). Knowledge management and collaboration create knowledge sharing. *Baseline Magazine.* Retrieved from http://www.baselinemag.com/c/a/Intelligence/Knowledge-Manage-ment-and-Collaboration-Create-Knowledge-Sharing- 513230/.

Devaney, L. (2009, July 22). Let retiring 'boomers' transform schools. *eSchoolNews.* Retrieved from http://www.eschoolnews.com/2009/07/22/let-retiring-boomers-transform-schools/.

Drucker, P. F. (1993). *Post-capitalist society.* New York: HarperCollins.

Gallup. (2009). *Parents rate schools much higher than do Americans overall.* Retrieved from http://www.gallup.com/poll/122432/parents-rate-schools-higher-americans-overall.aspx.

Gates Foundation. (2010). *This school works for me: Creating choices to boost achievement. A guide for America's school leaders.* Seattle: Author.

Greenberg, E. H., with K. Weber. (2008). *Generation WE: How millen-nial youth are taking over America and changing our world forever.* Emeryville, CA: Pachatusan.

Hais, M. D., & Winograd, M. (2008, February 3). The boomers had their day: Make way for the millennials. *The Washington Post.* Retrieved from http://www.washingtonpost.com/wp-dyn/content/article/2008/02/01/AR2008020102826.html.

Hargittai, E., Fullerton, L., Menchen-Trevino, E., & Thomas, K. (2010, April 22). Trust online: Young adults' evaluation of web content. *International Journal of Communication.* Retrieved from http://ijoc.org/ojs/index.php/ijoc/article/view/636/423.

Herbst, J. (1996). *The once and future school: Three hundred and fifty years of American secondary education.* New York: Routledge.

Holland, S. (2009, September 10). Despite push, year round schools get mixed grades. *CNN*. Retrieved from http://www.cnn.com/2009/US/09/04/us.year.round.schools/index.html.

Houle, D. (2008). *The Shift Age*. Charleston, SC: Booksurge.

Howe, N. (2010). Meet Mr. and Mrs. Gen X: A new parent generation. *The School Administrator, 1*(67). Retrieved from http://www.aasa.org/SchoolAdministratorArticle.aspx?id=11122.

IBM. (2010). *Capitalizing on complexity: Insights from the global chief executive officer study*. Somers, NY: Author.

Johnson, J., & Rochkind, J., with A. N. Ott & S. DuPont. (2009). *With their whole lives ahead of them: Myths and realities about why so many students fail to finish college*. New York: Public Agenda.

Jukes, I., McCain, T., & Crockett, L. (2010). *Living on the future edge: Windows on tomorrow*. Kelowna, British Columbia, Canada: 21st Century Fluency Project Inc.

Kotter, J. P. (1996). *Leading change*. Boston: Harvard Business School Press.

Lardinois, F. (2010, February 18). The most popular YouTube videos and the bloggers who embed them. *ReadWriteWeb*. Retrieved February 22, 2011 from http://www.readwriteweb.com/archives/whats_hot_on_youtube_and_who_is_embedding_those_vi.php

Manzo, K. K. (2009, August 31). Filtering fixes. *Education Week*. Retrieved from http://www.edweek.org/ew/articles/2009/09/02/02filter_ep.h29.html?tkn=QN[FwPR%2BcQ5C163IrJXxrec3ENEZu1KEL9H9.

Marshall, S. P. (2006). *The power to transform: Leadership that brings learning and schooling to life*. San Francisco: Jossey-Bass.

Medina, J. (2008). *Brain rules: 12 principles for surviving and thriving at work, home, and school*. Seattle: Pear Press.

National Center for Education Statistics. (n.d.). *School building statistics*. Retrieved from http://www.edfacilities.org/ds/statistics.cfm#.

Negroponte, N. (1995). *Being digital*. New York: Knopf.

New problem for unions: The rise of the white collar worker. (1959, January 5). *Time*. Retrieved from http://www.time.com/time/magazine/article/0,9171,810844,00.html.

Partnership for 21st Century Skills (2008). *21st century skills education & competitiveness: A resource and policy guide*. Washington, DC: Author.

Pew Research Center. (2006, December 16). Luxury or necessity? *Pew Research Center Publications*. Retrieved from http://pewresearch.org/pubs/323/luxury-or-necessity.

Pew Research Center. (2009). Generational differences in online activities. *Pew Internet & American Life Project*. Retrieved from http://pewinternet.org/Reports/2009/Generations-Online-in-2009/

Generational-Differences-in-Online-Activities/Generations-Explained.aspx?r=1.

Pew Research Center. (2010). *The Millennials: Confident. Connected. Open to change.* Retrieved from http://pewresearch.org/millennials/.

Pink, D. (2005). *A whole new mind: Moving from the information age to the conceptual age.* New York: Riverhead Books.

Prensky, M. (2010). *Teaching digital natives: Partnering for real learning.* Thousand Oaks, CA: Corwin.

RAND. (2003). *Are schools facing a shortage of qualified administrators?* (RAND Research Brief: RB-8021-EDU). Santa Monica, CA: Author.

Robinson, K. (2007, December 6). *Do schools kill creativity?* [Video file] Retrieved from http://www.youtube.com/watch?v=iG9 CE55wbtY.

Siemens, G. (2004). *Connectivism: A learning theory for the digital age.* Retrieved from http://www.elearnspace.org/Articles/con nectivism .htm.

Some schools grouping students by skill, not grade level. (2010, July 5). *USA Today.* Retrieved from http://www.usatoday.com/news/education/2010–07–05-grade-held-back_N.htm.

Strauss, B., & Howe, N. (1992). *Generations: The History of America's Future, 1584 to 2069.* New York: Harper Perennial.

Timeline of historic inventions (n.d.). In *Wikipedia.* Retrieved from http://en.wikipedia.org/wiki/Timeline_of_historic_inventions.

Toffler, A., & Toffler, H. (2006). *Revolutionary Wealth.* New York: Knopf.

Transformation. (n.d.) In *Dictionary.com.* Retrieved from http://dic tionary.reference.com/browse/transformation.

U.S. Department of Education, National Center for Education Statistics. (2007). *Beginning postsecondary students longitudinal study.* Retrieved from http://nces.ed.gov/pubsearch/pubsinfo.sp?pubid=2007041.

U.S. Department of Education, National Center for Education Statistics. (2008). *School size.* Retrieved from http://nces.ed.gov/pro grams/digest/d08/tables/dt08_096.asp.

U.S. Department of Education, National Center for Education Statistics. (2009a). *Numbers and types of public elementary and secondary schools from the common core of data: School year 2007–08.* Retrieved from http://nces.ed.gov/pubs2010/2010305.pdf.

U.S. Department of Education, National Center for Education Statistics. (2009b). *Special analysis 2009: International assessments.* Retrieved from http://nces.ed.gov/programs/coe/2009/analysis/index.asp.

U.S. Department of Labor, Bureau of Labor Statistics. (2008, June 27). *Number of jobs held, labor market activity, and earnings growth among the youngest baby boomers: results from a longitudinal survey* (Press Release). Retrieved from www.bls.gov/news.release/pdf/nlsoy .pdf.

U.S. Green Building Council (n.d.). *Presentations.* Retrieved from http://www.usgbc.org/DisplayPage.aspx?CMSPageID=1720.

Van Buskirk, E. (2010, May 17). 5-year-old YouTube tops networks' primetime with 2 billion views. *Wired.* Retrieved February 22, 2011, from http://www.wired.com/epicenter/2010/05/five-year-old-youtube-tops-networks-primetime-with-2-billion-views/.

Von Drehle, D. (2010, July 22). The case against summer vacation. *Time.* Retrieved from http://www.time.com/time/nation/article/0,8599,2005654,00.html.

Wagner, T. (2008). *The global achievement gap: Why even our best schools don't teach the new survival skills our children need—and what we can do about it.* New York: Basic Books.

Willingham, D. (2010, August 9). What's missing from common core standards, Part 3. *Washington Post.* Retrieved from http://voices.washingtonpost.com/answer-sheet/daniel-willingham/willingham-whats-missing-from-2.html.

YouTube Facts & Figures (history & statistics). (2010, May 17). Retrieved February 22, 2011, from http://www.website-monitoring.com/blog/2010/05/17/youtube-facts-and-figures-history-statistics/.

Index

CORWIN

A SAGE Company

The Corwin logo—a raven striding across an open book—represents the union of courage and learning. Corwin is committed to improving education for all learners by publishing books and other professional development resources for those serving the field of PreK–12 education. By providing practical, hands-on materials, Corwin continues to carry out the promise of its motto: **"Helping Educators Do Their Work Better."**